SILENCE SONG AND SHADOWS

OUR *NEED*
FOR THE SACRED
IN
OUR
SURROUNDINGS

TOM BENDER

FIRE RIVER PRESS

PUBLISHED BY ———

FIRE RIVER PRESS
PO Box 397
Manzanita OR 97130 USA
email: fireriverpress@nehalemtel.net

*This book is published
as an introductory visual companion volume to
BUILDING WITH THE BREATH OF LIFE,
which contains more detailed information on
energetics of place, its history, and use.*

FIRE RIVER PRESS books by the same author:

ENVIRONMENTAL DESIGN PRIMER, 1973
THE HEART OF PLACE, 1993
SILENCE, SONG, AND SHADOWS, 2000
BUILDING WITH THE BREATH OF LIFE, forthcoming 2000

LIBRARY OF CONGRESS CARD NUMBER 99-95598
Bender, Tom
    SILENCE, SONG, and SHADOWS:
    Our Need for the Sacred in Our Surroundings /
    by Tom Bender
    Includes bibliographical references
ISBN 0-9675089-0-8
       1. Body, Mind & Spirit – New Thought
       2. Feng-Shui – General
       3. Architecture – Sustainability & Ecological Design
       4. Health & Fitness – Healing
       5. Science – Chi Energy
       6. House & Home – Design and Caretaking

IN THANKS

It is humbling to realize how little actually comes from ourselves in what we do. To read again something from a half-forgotten friend or teacher from years ago, and realize how a seed quietly planted has grown over the years. To find how broad and deep the net of support is that life has brought us through the vehicle of family, friends, those marching to very different drummers, and other life that has merely touched us in passing. To know the others that have come before us upon whose work our own builds. To feel the footprints of others who have passed through virgin territory before, along with, or behind us, and see the paths that we have forged together. To discover the support and guidance from the spirit world that comes through our every dream, thought, and action.

We truly are as One, and the world that we are together dreaming into being becomes more awesome every day.

My heartfelt thanks goes out to all of the strands of Creation that have helped in the evolution of this project - they are too many and too interwoven to single out. In particular, however, my thanks for the wisdom and support given my by my sons, Morgan and Skye, and my wife, Lane deMoll; the hands-on guidance in the realms of chi by Dana Zia; the steadfast support in the process of birthing by David Rousseau, Carol Venolia, and Marc Rosenbaum; Jerry Horovitz' deep faith in the project; the wonderful assistance of research librarians Diane Niflis and Christine de Vallet in accessing materials from a rural location; the research assistance of Joey Korn and Sig Lonegren; technical assistance from Mark Beach; and the members of my local community. And, unforgettably, the mischievous presence and guidance from the builders of Angkor.

CONTENTS

1

OUR NEED FOR THE SACRED
IN OUR SURROUNDINGS

Silver Falls SP, Oregon

2

Sacredness has to do with our everyday world. It is not a once-a-week kind of thing. It underlies, but is distinct from, the religious expressions of the sacred which often tend to separate us from others with different spiritual traditions. Whenever we allow ourselves to know a place, person, or thing intimately, we come to love them. We see among their inevitable warts and wrinkles the special and wonderful things that they are, and their existence becomes as precious to us as our own. Loving them, we come to hold their existence inviolate - or sacred - and any action which would harm them becomes inconceivable. Openness, intimacy, knowledge, and love are the essential foundations upon which any healthy existence must be built.

We often consider the sacred something "optional" and nonessential to our surroundings. We find it difficult to conceive of the value to our communities of creating sacred places and holding them inviolate. We seem puzzled as to what real benefits would be gained by spending money to enrich our homes, public buildings, and community places with beautiful hand-crafted work. We seem confused as to what we would personally gain from changing our work and our workplaces to *enrich* skills and embody supportive values rather than minimizing the use of skill and the costs of our surroundings.

We ignore the sacred today because we fail to see the commonality in the many illnesses that arise from its absence in our lives. We ignore it also because we fail to understand the mechanisms by which the sacred affects and nurtures our lives and our health. We see ourselves surrounded by apparently intractable social problems - violence, alcoholism, drug use, crime, child abuse, apathy,

Expression of the sacred is incipient in all places.

Rock-cut temple, Ellora - India

failing schools. All are reaching epidemic proportions. All seem resistant to resolving.

These are not, however, separate problems. They are all symptoms of disease - not in our bodies -but in our psychic "immune systems" which keep always-present situations from escalating into epidemic problems. These social problems all arise out of the same lack of self-worth, lack of respect by and for others, or lack of opportunity to be of use and value to family and society. These problems are all a single *disease of the spirit*. Restoring the sacred in our lives is essential to healing this disease of the spirit, because it nurtures these very aspects of our relationships whose diminishment has resulted in these seemingly separate problems. In nurturing our souls, the sacred is central to sustainability of society and the ecological health of our planet. And it is the core of a meaningful existence.

This *disease of the spirit* is the same one we see in the eyes of people who have been defeated - individually or as a society - and who have seen what they love and value destroyed, lost, or taken away. It is the same disease of the spirit when wealth and comfort make us too self-satisfied to reach out for the vital nourishment and understanding arising from work, community, and giving to others. It is the same disease of the spirit where we lack the nurture of meaningful and honored goals, roles, responsibilities and power.

3

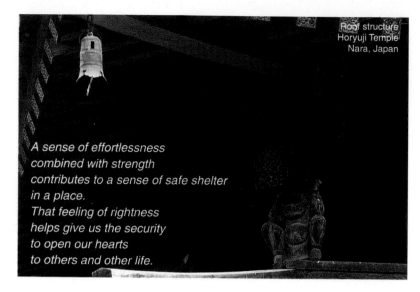

Roof structure
Horyuji Temple
Nara, Japan

*A sense of effortlessness
combined with strength
contributes to a sense of safe shelter
in a place.
That feeling of rightness
helps give us the security
to open our hearts
to others and other life.*

The sacred in our surroundings is essential for our well-being. We cannot have strong and clear intention that leads to real success in our lives unless all parts of our lives have coherence and resonate with the same core values. As our surroundings concretely reflect the values which were inherent in their making, it is essential that we bring both our places and our values into coherence as they reflect back into our lives.

Simply put, the sacred deals with "honoring". It deals with respect and reciprocity - with what the Christian Golden Rule distilled into, *"Do unto others as you would have them do unto you."* Honoring the sacred restores us to the wholeness needed to reconnect with our own hearts, our neighbors, and the world around us. It give us the strength to summon our vital inner resources and to guide the powerful tools of our technology into right paths.

The sacred teaches us the value of community- and ecologically-based economics, and including in our decisions costs passed on to others. It helps us understand the importance of "fair trade", rather than "free trade" whose only freedom is that of exploiting the less powerful. It

gives us the basis for transforming and creating institutions which work to support rather than deplete the lasting supply of world resources, biosystem health, and the capabilities of human and global systems that constitute our real wealth.

And finally, we have a need for the sacred in our surroundings because it is how our universe operates. Evolution (and life) requires a dynamic balance and tension between stability and stasis on one hand, and emergence of new and potentially harmful possibilities on the other. Love, giving, and holding sacred are the glue which maintains and holds together this churning, chaotic dance. If we deny the existence and role of vital aspects of our universe, we are asking for problems!

> *Sustainability requires a true transformation of our basic values, the development of a spiritual core to our lives and society, and a building of institutions that direct our actions in harmony with these values.*

Like a garden, our lives need to be weeded if they are to produce a good crop. Spiritual values are excellent cultivating tools. With them we become clearly aware how our conventional world splits us through the heart. We divide our time and lives between work and leisure. But rarely do we allow our work the leisure to be enriching. And rarely do we allow our leisure the purpose and reward of doing things of value and benefit. In a world of such contradictory values, wholeness is not possible.

How *do* we honor each other, ourselves, and the world which surrounds us? How do we honor old people, children, the sick or dying? How do we honor workers and those outside the workplace? How do we honor life's changes? How do we honor our neighbors, our past, our communities, or our adversaries? How do we honor plants and animals; the earth, air and waters; our planet and the stars from which we are descended? And how do we honor all these things in how we make and use our surroundings? Expressing a sense of honoring in our surroundings is but a small piece of a sacred world, but one which permeates and connects to everything. And it is one which constantly surrounds us with concrete images of what we value.

All economics, and all cultures and communities derive from distinctive assertions of value. If the values chosen reflect consumption, greed, and violence, they create a far different world than if those values derive from the sacred. E.F. Schumacher, in his path-breaking *"Buddhist Economics"* remarked on the characteristic kind of economics which arises from the values of Buddhism - on the role and importance of enriching work, of obtaining the maximum well-being from minimum consumption, and of the importance of non-attachment to wealth. He has shown also its effectiveness in creating successful life, culture, and tools.

Reestablishing a value base to our communities involves discovery of the real meaning of a whole range of sustainable values tied to the sacred. *Austerity*, for example, is important. It does not, as we might think, exclude richness or enjoyment. What it does do is help us be aware of things which distract us from our real goals in life.

When we understand austerity, we see that affluence has a great hidden cost. Its endless possibilities

demand impossible commitments of time and energy. It fails to discriminate between what is wise and useful and what is merely possible. We end up foregoing things necessary for a truly satisfying life to make time and space for trivia. As we relearn the value of austerity, along with stewardship, permanence, responsibility, enoughness, work, and interdependence, we create a new and enduring kind of community.

Garden
Neahkahnie, Oregon

Austerity in a garden.
A single plant can focus our attention on its wonder
in a way that would be obscured
in a garden of many plants.

5

The pathways by which the sacred affects our lives are many, varied and sometimes unfamiliar. It affects our bodies in giving us the security of support and nurture by others and obviating the tension of solitary responsibility. It affects our hearts by balancing the ever-present negative emotions of life with the healing and supportive emotions of love, caring, and being of value. It affects our minds through making visible the positive interactive pathways through which all life cares for us. And it affects our souls through direct connection with the souls of all Creation.

One of the least familiar but most important mechanisms by which our health is affected is through the vehicle of chi or life force energy, which provides generative and nurturing energy to our lives. The influence of chi between us and our surroundings works both directions. Our internal chi energy impacts and alters the energy of the places we inhabit, and in much the same way, the energy of the places themselves affects us.

Intimately related to chi is the role played by our intention, which is vital in directing and focusing chi energy. Intention also works independently in giving coherence and focus to

our actions in the shaping and use of our surroundings, and in their ability to embody our values and dreams. Any action inspired by love, for example, conveys that love and the importance of it to others.

Ritual, experience, and our patterns of use of places are vital in giving depth of meaning to our experiences and in bringing visible commitment and embodiment to our values and beliefs. They affect our experience, our places themselves, and the energetic interchange between us and our places. It is an important vehicle in invoking change in chi energy, opening us to the spirit world, and sustaining community health.

Embodiment of core values or of actual spiritual manifestations in design elements and energized symbols provides yet another means by which our surroundings can bring us in contact with the sacred. Unfamiliar to our culture, this has been an important tool in virtually all other cultures.

A final way that the sacred can affect us through our surroundings is when, because of their innate nature, design, or use, they become portals through which we can access the wisdom and support of the spirit world.

Outdoor Zendo
Farallones Institute
Occidental, California

Meditation cushions next to a rock invite us to pause, catch our breath, ground, and connect with the sacred within us.

We are clearly not distinct and separated from the world within which we move. Influence and awareness move both ways across our skins and entwine us and the rest of the universe into a single organism. The harm we cause to our surroundings returns to cripple and diminish our own lives. In this kind of world, there is no excuse for *taking* from our neighbors and surroundings. There is only reason upon reason for *giving* and enriching life on both sides of our skin. The implications for how we shape and use our surroundings and our lives are immense.

Giving, as a basis of action towards our surroundings, opens immense new possibilities. When designers or clients stop saying only what "I want..." in a project and start asking, "What can this *give*?", we begin to find exciting new opportunities to strengthen the web of community in our cities. Planting street trees gives pedestrian shelter and lessens summer heat for the whole community. Building placement can create useful outside public spaces. An inexpensive public walkway or bridge may create pedestrian connections between parts of a city. Proper juxtaposition of uses can encourage community and 24-hour life in our cities.

> *Our surroundings themselves are worthy of honoring. They give vital support to our lives. They give us joy and beauty, and have lives and souls in their own right. They also express our values and convey to others our inner strengths and fears, pride and hungers.*

They speak of our relation with nature. They reflect our patterns of work and what we do or don't gain from that work. They show our relations with others, and what paths we take to self-respect, balance, and growth.

They tell how we build, live and love, and our goals as a society. They show if we know ourselves as part of the great and all-encompassing drama and adventure of our universe, or if we see ourselves apart from it all. What they reflect back to us today is not inspiring.

Effort spent in enrichment of a place reflects the value we place on the activities it shelters. It can help create a powerful setting for the everyday rituals of life

House of the Living Goddess, Khatmandu, Nepal

The shaping of our surroundings can be a tool for healing ourselves and our relations to others. In a sacred society our surroundings become a source of meaning, power and strength which we lack today. To make our surroundings better, our hearts need to be in a better place - which we are learning step by step. If our surroundings are better, they make us better. Strength leads to vitality, just as weakness leads to impotence.

Sacred places and sacred building are vital to a healthy society. We all know of places which have such power for us. What is enshrined there is not necessarily something inherent in the places themselves, but, most potently, *our act* of holding something sacred. That act of holding sacred is key to healthy relationships which can sustain both us and our surroundings.

7

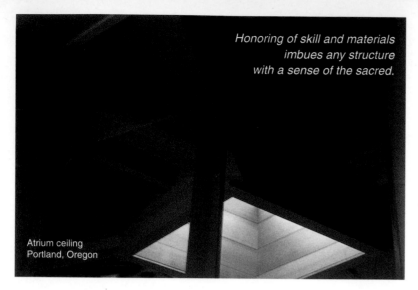

*Honoring of skill and materials
imbues any structure
with a sense of the sacred.*

Atrium ceiling
Portland, Oregon

We know in our own lives that if a person/place/ world we love is not happy, we can't be happy. *We soon discover that our well-being is dependent in large part on our contribution to the well-being of others* and of all life. As we reach out and come to know our world more intimately, we come to love each piece of it, and hold it sacred. This leads, inevitably, to discovering the sacredness of *all* places, *all* things, and *all* life; approaching all life in a sacred manner; and inhabiting, therefore, a sacred world. As part of a sacred world, we ourselves - individually and collectively - are to be held sacred also. And that calls forth a totally different way of relating and acting.

In a world that cherishes and holds sacred *all* life, there is no room for taking for greed rather than for need. In it we rediscover the multiple benefits of giving and sharing, and the healing nurture of relationships based on love and the sacred. This implements fundamental change in our ways of working, playing, celebrating, sharing, and shaping our surroundings. We find a new strength and vitality arising in all parts of our lives.

*T*he first step to both sound community and sound *design is to reaffirm the sacredness of our world and establish that value as a touchstone of our society.*

8

Life in a sacred society is difficult for many to comprehend, for we now have little sense of the kind of support, strength, freedom, meaning, and confidence - and therefore health - that arise from being part of a community of respect.

One dimension of it can be seen in a Quaker or Japanese community, where consensus and shared decision-making, shared responsibility, and respect for others is still a central strength. Other dimensions can be seen in indigenous communities throughout the world which still maintain ancient ties to land, spirit, and wholeness, and in the surroundings and patterns of life which have been shaped by such traditions. This different world comes into being as ripples outward from even the simplest act of bringing the sacred into our lives and our surroundings.

There is opportunity in every act of building to honor and show reverence. A spiritual base brings often subtle, but powerful, changes. A window rather than a mirror over a bathroom sink greets us in the morning with a view into a garden rather than a discouraging look at our outsides in their worst condition. It stops the diminishment of self-esteem that mirrors give. It helps wean us from excessive attention to the surface qualities of things.

Putting a "1% for heart" clause in construction contracts for builder ideas to enhance the environmental, esthetic and spiritual quality of a project can end up making *all* of the project better while simultaneously enriching workers' skills and self-esteem. Natural materials can honor their sources. Creating silence and shadow in our places can give breathing room for users and space for new creation to occur.

Our places need to convey a spirit of greatness in our hearts, of celebration of the universe we inhabit and of our connection with it. We need to create homes for our spirits as well as our activities. We need to express the special spirit of every place and our own unique time in our surroundings - and to celebrate the rain, the winter, the night, the heat - and find ways to live comfortably in harmony with them.

The power of place has always been in the realm of its meaning, and its ability to align and marshal the invisible inner forces of our spirits with the invisible forces of nature. Spirit and sacredness are the root of that power; and place, not space, its manifestation.

Sometimes we may stumble onto one of those rare places that bring us into powerful contact with the primal forces of our world - a remote farmhouse, a forgotten temple garden, a simple barn, or possibly a famous cathedral. They make our hearts overflow in the same way as does a grove of ancient redwoods or a mountain-top sunrise. We know then with certainty that the surroundings we create *can* and *should* powerfully move our hearts. They can give deep

All places hold stories of their makers – their dreams, their achievements, the wonder of the universe they dreamed into being.

Erechtheion
Athens, Greece

nourishment to our lives and provide us with concrete visions of what is needed and possible in all our actions. We can, without question, create places with a soul.

It is time to put heart back into our places.

Communities, too, have personalities and reflect their makers. Present efforts to improve the sustainability of our society have so far ignored the vital human and spiritual components of enduring patterns. A city can have the best conceivable design of green space, homes, neighborhoods, efficient transportation, and material- and energy-efficient construction. That does not make it capable of moving our hearts.

It is our dreams, our passions, our distinctive cultures and ways of life that give shape to our cities and give them the power to move our hearts and affect our lives. We can live without wealth, but not without love and meaning.

We need places we can love, and enjoy, and about which we can be fervent. We need to rediscover how to make the communities where we live able to raise our passions and move our hearts.

Part of the specialness of places that touch our hearts are those unique qualities - climate, geology, history and community of inhabitants that make a place distinctively different from others and which gives root to a unique personality and spirit in its inhabitants.

Esalen Institute
Big Sur, California

A peaceful community meditation garden created from only a basin of water and a few rocks.

The "Paradise Gardens" of Isfahan give a unique sense of its desert world. The incredible water and temple systems of the Khmers harnessed river floods to supply water for a sustainable agriculture, tied it into the cosmology of their beliefs and provided for the distribution of chi throughout the kingdom. The Winter Cities of Canada

have grasped the power of imagery, meaning and emotion of winter living and transformed their communities into wonderful celebrations of winter with ice skating, winter festivals, skiing, snowmobiling and sled dog races.

An enduring wonder graces a village like Amien or Mt. St. Michael in France, or places like Chichen Itza in Mexico, where a quest for expression of the exultation of life and creation has transformed an entire community into a magical manifestation of that power. That wonder is possible in *our* communities as well.

Power of place can arise from layer after layer of the simple everyday acts of everyday people, as well as from great inspiration. Many towns and villages have an evening tradition of the "passerada", where people gather in outdoor cafes and in the squares and enjoy the spectacle of the young and old eyeing each other, making overtures, beginning and renewing friendships. Out of this grows depth and sustenance of tradition and community. Amish villages and farm country show an indelible mark of their continuing nurture of life, as do Swiss mountain villages where traditions of vibrant flower boxes in every window have evolved, giving a special spirit to even the simplest village.

Love of a place can even evolve invisibly out of our simple but fundamental act of *belonging* to it. Some Native American tribes bury a rock during their ceremonies of founding a new village. The rock is not necessarily in the middle of the planned village, or a special rock, or prominently visible. It is important, however, as marking an action establishing commitment and relationship.

It says, "In this place we will live. Our lives will be centered here, and we will see the universe and our surroundings from this point. Our lives here are a connection with this place." And out of that kind of commitment arises a sense of connection with a meaningful, valued and loved place. In a related way, the great cities of China, India, Egypt, or Mesoamerica have been built upon an image of the cosmos, the nation, nature, and our place within it, which gives unique and potent meaning to the lives of their inhabitants.

Our lives are sustained through our hearts being moved by the places where we live and visit. The power of those places evokes a similar will to self-esteem, to dreaming great dreams, and to the will to achieve them. We can transform our communities into something which draws forth the love of residents and visitors alike - in the physical fabric of the city, in the celebrations it supports and nurtures, and the way of life it empowers.

A community which lives only for the greed of commerce and consumption does not enjoy itself, and does not enjoy life. It has no great passions, and dreams only small dreams. Such a community has not learned the great drama of life of which we are part, and is not capable of creating sustaining bonds within itself, with its neighbors, and with the natural world in which it is embedded.

It is human passions and failings, dreams and hardship, that dominate the spirit of place of communities and give them the power to arouse our feelings and our will to maintain, refine, and enrich them, and to ensure their life into the future.

Taking part ourselves in the making of a thing deepens its meaning to us. A totem pole carved by students and parents greets visitors to an Oregon school.

Make our communities places to love. That is the sustaining force of life. When we have communities we are passionate about and which nurture our souls, we will want them to endure. With that love, we will seek and assure the changes in infrastructure, land use, building practices and patterns of living essential to that survival.

11

BUILDING WITH THE
BREATH OF LIFE

2

Necarney Creek, Oregon

Studio window
Neahkahnie, Oregon

Our surroundings act as mirrors, truly reflecting the values, dreams, fears, and fascinations of the individuals and societies that have shaped them. We can, if we wish, read them like a book, pointing out item by item what was in the minds and hearts of those who created and shaped a place.

An interesting curiosity. Yet more than that. These images in stone and steel, those dreams in faded neon and spalling stucco deeply affect and shape us. They affect us as strongly even as they in their turn were affected and shaped by their makers.

—— They affect us in part because they convey the true fears behind our painted smiles, the cruelty behind the benign surfaces of actions, the love behind the modest gesture.

—— They affect us because they clarify and embody our dreams, marshaling our inner resources to their achievement.

—— They affect us as they show, often with a beauty or ugliness which makes their message even more poignant, the confusions of our goals, the inconsistency of our actions, the humanness of our lives.

—— They affect us because they do not lie, and stand witness to our lives as they are - in their fullness or in their emptiness.

Imagine what it would have been like to be a 19th century architect in Rome, surrounded by two thousand years of the greatest masterpieces of the Roman Empire and the Italian Renaissance. Quite an achievement to live up to or be measured against. Some might have been encouraged to do their greatest, inspired by the achievements of their ancestors. Many others gave up before they began, feeling incompetent in comparison. Whole societies have fallen into the doldrums in such cases, stifled by the context of history.

Consider what the physical environment of most public housing says to its residents - of bureaucratic bungling, lack of caring for our physical, emotional and spiritual well-being, and disregard of community. It speaks of warehousing "problem people", of crime, and lack of love or caring for surroundings. Think what it says to its residents of the basic value of greed and inequity that made even provision of minimal housing impossible for so many. There is no question that people's lives in such places are weighted down by what their surroundings tell them their society thinks of them.

13

In contrast, feel the inspiration that was given the entire community by the transcendental beauty and power of a Gothic cathedral in a French village, or what the tree-lined boulevards and sidewalk cafes in European cities create today as support for community life.

Fire escapes
Chicago, Illinois

*What we dream is
what we get.*

The *consistency* between our beliefs and our actions which our surroundings reflect is also important. A university computer science department may talk about how its work is transforming society, eliminating need for work spaces. If they then submit a plan for new facilities for themselves, filled with standard faculty offices and classrooms like every other university building, their claims become unbelievable to others, and eventually to themselves.

The way our surroundings reflect our values usually occurs unconsciously and without direct attention. But in those rare times when society is undergoing fundamental change, we suddenly see the disparities and implications of our beliefs and actions, and can actively move to establish new touchstones in both.

Today is one of those times. We are beginning to see through the contradictions in our sciences and beliefs to a deeper and clearer basis for our lives. In the process, a new and clearer sense of the role of the sacred in our surroundings and a new operative vision of how it affects us is emerging. Interestingly, this is occurring at the same time as the fundamental nature of the society is undergoing an elemental change from a growth orientation to one which can be sustained over long periods of time.

One of the unexpected new elements of this understanding of the sacred has to do with chi energy. This new element has emerged strongly in health and healing, but also in the sciences, and in the arts of relationships among people, place and things. Verifiable through our own senses, giving deeper and more fecund power to our awareness of self and touching of our outer world, this new vision is transforming all aspects of our perception, experience and living.

The world of chi is at once new and timelessly ancient. It is a vision of the energy rather than material basis of all creation, of the intimate interconnectedness of all life. It is a vision of the rhythmic iteration of sound, of song, of complex vibration, harmonics and overtones, that give rise to and maintain all the complex interfolding structure of the universe.

Virtually every culture other than our own has experienced and incorporated an understanding of this *breath of life* into all aspects of their culture. Ours alone seems to have lost this understanding. *Chi, prahna, kundalini, ki, vis medicatrix naturae, mana*....the names are as many as the cultures which have known it, but the consistency and accuracy of the description and understanding is awesome. The personal experience of this breath of life through yoga, tai chi, qi-gong, martial arts, meditation, or spontaneous occurrences is acknowledged by increasing numbers in our own culture. We are experiencing it today with the same consistency and replicability as in past cultures.

Today also, we have arrived at the moment in time when the effects of our culture's values of greed, growth, and violence are becoming unsustainable and when they must be released. It is wonderfully apt that at this very moment a new, clear, and powerfully appropriate vision is emerging upon which to base the transformation of our lives to ones of sustainability, giving, and love.

The bells, music, liturgy, stained glass, physical size and beauty of Amiens Cathedral infuse its entire community with a shared sense of the sacred.

The values of a greed- and growth-centered society have forced us to build walls around our hearts to isolate ourselves from the bitter pain and anguish resulting from what our culture dreams into being around us. That isolation, in turn, has created its own inner pain, as well as surroundings of inconceivable emptiness and meaninglessness.

15

Our ways of building - what we call today architectural, landscape, interior, urban and regional design and their allied construction arts - are constantly redefined in our minds and hearts in every era, as those arts and our values co-evolve. In Gothic France they were the means of expressing heavenly harmony and radiance.

During the Enlightenment in Europe, they were an expression of the power of reason and order of mathematics. In the 19th century, a celebration of the ability of an industrial culture to transform and tame nature. In our lifetimes alone, architecture has been redefined from decade to decade as a visual art, a means of self-expression, the business of design, the packaging of development, and now as a plethora of incoherent neo-this and post-thats.

In the process, dimension after dimension of meaning and power have been stripped from these arts. I remember even now my own bewilderment as a beginning design student thirty-five years ago, being asked to make an "abstract composition". There were unspoken rules, of course, for this, but even the most hallowed examples never moved my heart, held meaning, nor seemed an adequate basis for design. Similarly, over-fascination with expression of structure and concern with *space* rather than *place* reflect this same imbalance in meaning.

This systematic removal of meaning from the shaping of our surroundings has resulted in undue emphasis being given to what little remains. Esthetics, for example, is given great weight in current design work. Yet sources as ancient as the *I-Ching* specifically warn *against* such emphasis on esthetics:

*"Grace - beauty of form - is necessary in any union if it is to be well ordered and pleasing rather than disordered and chaotic. Grace brings success. **However, it is not the essential or fundamental thing; it is only the ornament and must therefore be used sparingly and only in little things.**"*

*"...beautiful form suffices to brighten and throw light upon matters of lesser moment, **but important questions cannot be decided in this way. They require greater earnestness.**"*

Esthetics is copying or measuring something against the past - against standards that we already hold within us from our culture. It is not part of any *living* art. A *living* art requires forging afresh a sense of wholeness and particular rightness in each act of creation.

Different aspects of this can be seen dramatically in Inuit "art" or Navajo and Tibetan sand painting, where the process of making is all and the product tossed aside on completion; in certain temple traditions in India, where once an offering of sculpture or architecture was completed, it was left to return to dust unrepaired; or in the Shinto temples in Japan, such as at Ise, where the ongoing total replacement of temple structures every twenty years keeps the work of the temple builders as a spiritual practice intact and alive.

Lack of deeper dimensions can turn landscape design, for example, into merely a cover-up for bad architectural design, or a visually pleasing setting for a building.

The Royal Mosque in Isfahan, Iran - for over 500 years a place of deep peace and spiritual presence.

It is extremely rare today that interior and exterior places are designed congruently to intensify experience of nature, or that gardens are designed specifically as places of nurture for our souls.

As our society moves from a period of growth into a period of mature sustainability, this new energy-based vision gives a powerful and appropriate guidance for transforming our placemaking arts. It gives an inner kernel of power to these arts out of which a deeper, richer, more meaningful, and more unified expression can unfold. It gives the means to create more bountiful surroundings in harmony with both our inner vision and our connection with all of Creation.

Perhaps a good way to get a feel for what we are lacking is to take a look at what distinguishes the art of placemaking in a culture which clearly acknowledged the central spiritual role of human actions and the core role of the breath of life. One of the few design frameworks from sustainable societies whose record has come down to us relatively intact is the Chinese practice of feng-shui.

Many sustainable societies did not practice codified design. Others restricted it to sacred, or religious structures. The record of others has been lost. We have chronicles of the *Vintana* in Madagascar and the Hindu

17

The strategic placement of tombs, cities, pagodas, and bridges to heighten the balance, clarity, and chi of the landscape is part of the Chinese practice of feng-shui.

Vastuvidya in India, as well as the systems of *feng-shui* in China. The design sciences from the Mayan world, though fascinating, are only now being reconstructed after the Spanish burning of records in the 1500's. The feng-shui history is unique, perhaps, in its extensive written documentation and its application to cities, temples, homes, interior design, and the landscape as a whole.

Feng-shui (literally "wind and water") is the traditional basis of Chinese placemaking arts. Chi is central to its practices. It speaks of locating favorable sites for buildings, cities, and tombs based on the flows and varying concentrations of chi energy in the earth.

Documentation of the sun's influence on electromagnetic fields in the earth's crust and atmosphere during the early space program showed that there is a verifiable geophysical basis to at least some parts of the feng-shui practices. Comprehension has also come together concerning other, more alien, aspects of its theory and practices. And, piece by piece, through twenty-five years of incorporating feng-shui principles into architectural practice in our culture, its application and mechanisms of operation have been demonstrated.

With the value of energetics of place demonstrated by feng shui, practices in other cultures which parallel feng-shui have been discovered. They have shown alternate ways to accomplish good energetics of place, or aspects of energy design not considered by the Chinese. What works in our culture is sometimes similar, sometimes different from that of the Chinese, Hindu, Buddhist, Mayan, Egyptian and other traditions.

Over several thousand years, feng-shui practice became separated from the active shaping and altering of place. It accreted layers of superstition and became focused on largely symbolic actions to improve the energy and power of place (not to belittle the effect of symbolic actions.) Yet its basic scope and content uniquely match the needs of reconceiving our design arts today. Reintegrating the kinds of principles it was based on into active design, and applying them freshly in a new cultural context gives us a good place to start in generating a much needed new wholeness, power, and rightness in our surroundings.

The basic principles of a sacred or subtle-energy based design system are found partially in the details and practices recorded in its books and manuals and taught by its masters. Perhaps more important to us, though, are the frequently unstated assumptions that underlie a range of specific rules and practices. These were so integral a part of the culture that no one considered the need for stating them. But to a totally different culture such as ours, they are essential to seeing the differentness and fundamental roots of sustainable design.

There are ten principles that systems such as feng-shui suggest underlie the practice of design in any sustainable society. For a person brought up in the beliefs of our society, some of these may initially seem strange, or their design significance difficult to grasp. Examples in later chapters should give a feel for their potential today.

---

10 PRINCIPLES OF A CHI-BASED SOCIETY

1. Life force energy, or CHI, underlies all Creation.

2. The energy fields of the earth are a source of energy and information to all living matter.

3. The breath of life, or "chi" exists in all people, places, and things, and is vital to their interaction.

4. The astrology of people and places, and the timing of their interaction play an active role in the outcome of those interactions.

5. The health of all Creation is essential to our well-being.

6. Our minds and hearts are an integral and powerful part of our interaction with the world on both sides of our skins, and must be addressed in design and use of place.

7. Our relationships with the past and the future - towards our ancestors and our descendants, what preceded us and what evolves out of our existence - are important to the outcome of interactions with our surroundings.

8. Harmony with our cosmology needs to be integral to the design of our surroundings.

9. Sacredness is central to meaningful lives and an enduring society,

10. Design and use of our surroundings are spiritual paths, based on love and giving.

L et's look in a little more detail at what these principles entail:

1. LIFE FORCE ENERGY, OR CHI, UNDERLIES ALL CREATION.

Our bodies and the physical world around us are particular patterns of matter that have gelled around specific matrices of chi energy. In this sense, our energy bodies are more primary than our physical ones, and the

Original reconstruction, headdress of Puabi, from Sumeria.

Chi is depicted in many cultures as emerging from the crown chakra, with representation of seven chakras.

The art of almost every culture has depicted the existence of chi energy.

20

processes and relationships there more basic than in our physical bodies. And they are profoundly interconnected.

Chi energy here is distinct from the electrical energy in a house that we plug our stereos into. It is the *life force*, *breath of life*, or *prahna* which has been the basis of healing, spiritual practices, and cultural organization for millennia. What this "energy" actually is remains unclear at this time, as our sciences are only beginning to examine it.

Contemporary experiences of chi fit exactly into the descriptions given in classical literature and living traditions. We can eagerly look forward to its clearer and more technical understanding and application. But the leadership role today is in experiencing and acknowledging its existence, its roles, our connections with it and discovering how its acceptance and use can transform our lives and culture. The other will follow.

Experience of this aspect of existence profoundly changes our view of our lives and our world. Energy flows through and nurtures our bodies except when we block it off. We experience our existence as nodes in a continuous interconnecting field of energy rather than discrete, separate objects. We feel our own chi performing what was long known as spiritual healing. We find ourselves so coherently interlinked with others that our thoughts and memories are one. We walk in the fields of incipient form where things and events take shape. Strange and unexpected new worlds open before us.

This energy dimension of existence is key to understanding esoteric practices of many cultures that we have found difficult to comprehend. The Australian Aborigines talk of healing broken bones within a few hours. Tibetan Buddhism *lung-gom* and *tum-mo* practitioners run with extraordinary swiftness over fields of boulders, and keep themselves warm in snow and ice without clothing.

The !Kung people of the Kalahari Desert in Africa practice a particular dance to "heat up" their *n/um*, or what the Hindus call *kundalini*, so that a *!kia* state of transcendence can be attained. In those dances, more than half of the tribe can attain such states. In the *!kia* state, extraordinary feats occur, such as curing the sick, walking on fire, or having remote vision allowing them to see over vast distances. Native American tribes use trance drumming to attain similar states.

Even today, hundreds of thousands of otherwise normal people in our own culture have experienced fire walking, acupuncture, shamanic journeying, and other practices which our sciences can't explain. The traditions of those practices have always stated, however, that they were tied to chi.

The role of our familiar material world in all of this is very different from a universe in which that material world was all that existed. And building design which acknowledges, responds to, and incorporates both of these worlds in their complex interaction is very different from merely creating pleasing spatial designs.

2. **THE ENERGY FIELDS OF THE EARTH ARE A SOURCE OF ENERGY AND INFORMATION TO ALL LIVING MATTER.**

The "solar wind" of energy particles interacts with the magnetic field of the earth, creating complex and dynamic electromagentic fields.

The visible light that fuels photosynthesis and supports all life on earth constitutes only a minute fraction of the Sun's energy that is intercepted by our planet. The "solar wind" is comprised of plasma radiations as well as electromagnetic waves. When intercepted by the Earth's magnetic field, the solar wind shapes the magnetosphere and the plasmasphere of our planet.

They, in turn induce much of that energy into the earth's atmosphere and mantle in the form of electro-magnetic energy. As those charged particles oscillate back and forth along the magnetic lines of the earth between the north and the south poles, their intensity is visible through the ionized gas effects of the northern and southern lights - the *aurora borealis* and the *aurora australialis*.

Much of this energy circles the earth in the resonant cavity of the atmosphere between the earth's surface and the ionosphere, creating a resonant frequency (called the Schumann resonance) at about 10 Hertz - the reciprocal of the time required for a beam of electromagnetic radiation to go around the earth. This is the same as one of the base resonant frequencies of our brain waves. Barbara Brennan and others indicate that a distinct type of energy connects our intentionality to the energy core of the earth and draws energy from it to support our lives and actions.

In turn, electromagnetic fields induced into the

mantle of the earth, and their variation due to topography and geology create variations in local electromagnetic fields.

Like any available energy source, these have been seized upon by the multitude of life forms that have emerged on this planet to fuel and inform their life. It remains a question today what of these "earth energies" consist of pulsed electromagnetic fields, and what of other forms of "energy". For now, we have to be satisfied in the knowledge that they have been and are apprehensible and useful.

In the same way as this vortex in the Mediterranean Sea off of Italy creates regions of unique energy, movement of chi in our surroundings results in areas of high and low energy concentration.

For millennia, "power spots" of these energies have been used by animals and humans - for birthing places and healing; for shrines and churches; for propitious location of cities, homes, temples and tombs. Divination, or dowsing, for temple siting is recorded in almost every culture.

Temples of some sects in India are built of bricks fired in place after the building was built. Constructed that way, the magnetic field orientations of each particle of clay of the bricks are in full alignment with that of the place at that time. No repairs or changes are permitted in these temples, to preserve that purity of alignment. They are allowed to fall to ruin in their own time, rather than alter the purity of the fields established in their making.

This is use of the chi of place for specific and sensitive human needs. Our everyday activities may, or may not, be as susceptible to such subtle effects of the natural chi of place.

3. *THE BREATH OF LIFE, OR "CHI" EXISTS IN ALL PEOPLE, PLACES, AND THINGS, AND IS VITAL TO THEIR INTERACTION.*

Chi is not just something in the ground or in our bodies. It permeates our surroundings as well - intensely in what are called sacred places, in good and bad concentrations elsewhere. Traditionally, virtually all cultures considered it in finding favorable locations for temples, shrines, homes, businesses, and tombs.

Of importance here is that the chi of people and place are interactive. Our chi alters the chi of places we use, and their chi alters our own. And the chi of *built* places and the human chi interacting with them is definitely strong enough to alter the lives of people using those places. The good or bad energy of users of a place linger to affect subsequent users. Our interaction with place is additive and cumulative. We need to both design and live our lives aware of this dialog.

4. *THE ASTROLOGY OF PEOPLE AND PLACES, AND THE TIMING OF THEIR INTERACTION PLAYS AN ACTIVE ROLE IN THE OUTCOME OF THOSE INTER-ACTIONS.*

The energy fields of the earth are influenced by heavenly bodies other than the sun, as well as by all life on earth, and possibly other realms of existence. In turn, they convey those influences onto our lives. In what ways and how powerfully this might affect the our lives through our use of places, or in what ways we can alter those effects is still poorly understood.

5. *THE HEALTH OF ALL CREATION IS ESSENTIAL TO OUR WELL-BEING.*

Our skins are not always a meaningful line of distinction between what is and is not "us". What is inside our skins depends upon myriad kinds of food, air, and nurture from outside our skin. What lies outside our skins depends equally on us as a source for CO_2 and for food. The health and well-being of what lies on either side of our skins cannot be separated from that of the other side.

Candles, paper prayers, chorten (pyramids of balanced rocks), or other tokens make directly visible to others the energy we bring to a place.

23

The ecological connectedness of all life means that the well-being of *all* life must be part of our designing in addition to things that influence our specific health and well-being. The health, richness, and latent creativity of our planet's biosystems is one of the most important elements of our wealth and assurance of future well-being.

When our numbers and our appetites press too hard, when our actions deprive other life, we are increasing our own poverty as well as harming and destroying other life. Other life is more than just a reservoir of unknown pharmaceuticals and DNA. It is a celebration of the richness and beauty of Creation. The fewer the voices, the more diminished the song.

It is not just our numbers, but an inner sense of connectedness which is affected. We create landscapes with visually appealing ornamental plants. Yet the "weeds" we eliminate are essential food or shelter for birds, butterflies, beetles, and spiders, and might even be useful for our own health.

Our rapid logging cycles destroy the unseen mycorrhizal fungal mats upon which the health and life of coniferous forests depend. Our freeways and fencing cut migration routes. Our pesticides kill the food of unforeseen species. Our monoculture lawns deplete the genetic bank of wild species. Our houses rarely have nesting places for birds and bats, or food supply for spiders.

24

A different awareness can change how we deal with all these issues. It allows us closeness with other life and the joy of being part of a particular ecological community and place.

Our health is part of the health of all Creation. Getting to know other life - from bats to spiders to slugs to fungus, we begin to see the different wonder of each life, and come to respect and protect it.

> **6.** *OUR MINDS AND HEARTS ARE AN INTEGRAL AND POWERFUL PART OF OUR INTERACTION WITH THE WORLD ON BOTH SIDES OF OUR SKINS, AND MUST BE ADDRESSED IN DESIGN AND USE OF PLACE.*

The psychology of our human and cultural nature - our values, our beliefs, our fears, our memories - all direct our actions along certain paths, and determine much of the satisfaction or unhappiness that results from our interaction with places. The surroundings we create inescapably reflect and make manifest these deepest and most hidden values.

Even in a business environment expenditures on making people happy are worthwhile. In most office buildings, measures which result in as little as a 3% increase in productivity more than pay back even a *doubling* of the cost of the building! Operable windows, natural daylight, human-scaled spaces, adjustable task lighting, and comfortable furniture are all part of such conditions. Design so that people aren't always worrying about the boss sneaking up behind them and checking on them is also part. Such "green" office design has now been shown to bring extremely profitable improvements to working places. But the real bottom line is that paying attention to our emotional needs makes us feel better.

How we feel about a place or a pattern of interaction with place is important. Yet we're never encouraged to trust our tummies, and the consideration of the psychological dimension of people and place is virtually non-existent today.

Simply stated, this principle says to listen to your feelings and trust your tummy. If a place doesn't feel good *to* you, it isn't good *for* you. If we can change how we feel about a place through ritual, or through real or symbolic changes in our surroundings, we change some aspects of how the place affects us. If, for instance, we let our surroundings show our honoring of others, it will deepen that honoring and reflect back onto us the importance of that value of caring.

It is telling that Christopher Alexander's *Pattern Language*, the strongest proponent and example of the value of following our noses and tummies, is shunned by mainstream design professionals.

> **7.** *OUR RELATIONSHIPS WITH THE PAST AND THE FUTURE - TOWARDS OUR ANCESTORS AND OUR DESCENDANTS, WHAT PRECEDED US AND WHAT EVOLVES OUT OF OUR EXISTENCE - ARE IMPORTANT TO THE OUTCOME OF INTERACTIONS WITH OUR SURROUNDINGS.*

It's common knowledge in ecological literature now that many traditional cultures consider the impacts of actions as far as seven generations into the future. They do this both to see the full impacts of those actions, and so as to not restrict the potentials of that future.

Living with the results of a society that has disregarded the immense long range costs of their actions, we can now see the wisdom of such a perspective. We invariably *do* receive what we dream of. And when we dream only of the present and ignore the future, we reduce the likelihood of even having a future.

Interestingly, at least one culture speaks of those seven generations differently - as three past, the present, and three future ones.

Why consider the past? What's gone is gone....or isn't it?

Perhaps not entirely. Consideration of the gifts from past generations results in humility, acknowledgment of the size of the shoulders upon which we stand, and gratitude for those gifts as a basis for our actions. It provides us a realization that our achievements do not belong to us alone, and requires acknowledgment of our obligation to pass equivalent gifts on to *our* descendants. Sustainability requires both of these perspectives on duration and relationship over time.

Many cultures assert that our ancestors are actually with us in the present moment. This, amazingly, is consistent with what we are learning today of energetics and the existence of non-material realms of our universe.

Research in more and more fields is supporting concepts of the non-linearity of time, of parallel universes, and the contiguous existence of past, present, and future. More connection seems to be occurring between embodied people and those whose existence currently is not on the material plane. Our understandings and awareness in this area are changing dramatically.

25

Grave, Fuchou
Fukien Prov., China

Set into the south side of a hill, protected on the north by trees, on the east and west by protective lions, and having a sun-filled terrace and pool of water to the south, this Chinese tomb has what is considered very auspicious feng shui. Such sites enhance the energy of descendents and provide portals to connect with the ancestors.

If we consider ourselves to be a part *of* ongoing creation rather than apart *from* it, we have very different attitudes towards the possibilities we foreclose or create for the future, as well as how we relate to the entire shape of an ever-evolving history. Having a future implies ongoing Creation.

8. *Harmony with our cosmology needs to be integral to the design of our surroundings.*

A world built upon contradictions and lacking inner harmony destroys itself in the inner battles between differing and competing values. If our beliefs lack consistency and harmony, how can we put the full power of our will behind them, to say nothing of asking others to believe in them?

If our surroundings *do* tap the emotional, intellec-

tual, and spiritual core of our beliefs, they gain great dominion, and imbue our lives with that same power of coherent and powerful belief.

Every age and culture has a different view of the universe and our place in it. One role of our surroundings, like the results of all of our actions, is to give form to and represent those unique beliefs. Within them, then, we have the opportunity and support to bring our lives into harmony with the cosmos we perceive.

The hierarchical order of a Chinese city, the sacred geometries of Islamic ornament, or the bold power of a 20th century skyscraper all reflect unique views of the universe, consistent with the beliefs and the world their builders dreamed into being. In doing so, such creations renew and strengthen the universe within which they are founded, and those who inhabit that universe.

Maurice Freedman speaks of the difference in the meaning of their surroundings to Europeans and Chinese enjoying a view. The Europeans think of the combination of hills and sea producing splendid vistas. Their pleasure is esthetic and objective, the landscape is "out there", and they enjoy it. The Chinese appreciation is cosmological. For them the viewer and the viewed are interacting, both being part of some greater system. The cosmos is Heaven, Earth, and Us. We are in it and of it. So while the European reaction is to find it beautiful, the Chinese may remark that they feel content or comfortable. Their philosophy asserts a human response to forces working in the cosmos, and just as landscapes affect us, we may affect them.

Our cosmology has become one of contradiction. We're asked to be rational and efficient in work, yet irrational and inefficient in consumption. We happily consume the very resources that are needed for continued support of our lives. A new sense of the cosmos and our role in it is both needed and emerging. If how we live, work, and govern ourselves is headed in a different direction from our innermost dreams, or fails to incorporate major elements of those dreams, we head for failure and trouble.

Public expression of sacredness is rare in modern society. Interestingly, there *is* one particular place where people publicly and powerfully express a palpable sense of spiritual reverence and awe, of yearning, and of wonder. It is the exhibit in the Smithsonian Institution in Washington DC where we can touch a piece of rock from the moon.

Our urge to embrace, be part of, and reunite with the cosmos is a primal and valid one. It may well not require the massive space program and physical travel between worlds envisioned in our first outward spasm. Yet how contrary to those dreams it is to live in the cities of our world where incessant electric day shuts out the night and we can't even *see* the stars!

Until our actions towards the stellar world come from a reverence in our hearts, we will not find a harmony between our dreams and our actions. When our vision of our universe has wholeness, we will see all that surrounds us as part of that wholeness. The *aurora borealis* will change from being a strange natural phenomena into a visible sign of the energy fluxes channeling into our planet through its poles, linking our own existences to the stars.

In the same way, our attitudes towards the sacredness of all Creation and all forms of life must come to the same fullness and rightness of expression.

Our world view is turning from one of taking, greed, and violence to one of harmony, sharing and nurture. As it does so, our surroundings must take on powerful expressions of those new qualities if they are to take part in our nurture and become part of a harmony between us and our universe.

> ## 9. SACREDNESS IS CENTRAL TO MEANINGFUL LIVES AND AN ENDURING SOCIETY.

Our society stresses freedom - absence of connectedness, responsibility, or effects of our actions. Ours is a legalistic society - of limited commitments easy to break, and with great incentives for those finding new ways to

27

*Where our hearts and values are as we touch our
surroundings determine what our surroundings become.*

take from others, or to harm and destroy the rest of creation. Fed by its own power of destructiveness, it cannot last, and cannot create an ongoing basis for sustainability.

The only true alternative is à basis for our lives which makes harmful action inconceivable rather than the

rule. And nothing less than our holding sacred the health of our surroundings and the well-being of others will ensure that we act strongly enough or soon enough to ensure that health and well-being.

> **10.** **DESIGN AND USE OF OUR SURROUNDINGS ARE SPIRITUAL PATHS, BASED ON LOVE AND GIVING.**

A sacred world requires that all relationships - including work - be based on patterns that support the health, well-being, and spiritual growth of all involved. The traditions of energetics of place and sacred building demonstrate how design work and building, specifically, can be pursued as a process of spiritual growth of the practitioners as well as being an integral part of a sacred society. What we design can only reflect what we *are*, so a sacred society requires work processes that nurture our own spiritual health and growth.

This implies work patterns that support and encourage the development and enrichment of skills. It implies design and building processes that honor and encourage the creative contributions of the makers and users, that honor the life of materials given up into our construction; that honor all forms of life.

Together, these principles constitute and reflect a world view and basis of design profoundly different from what currently exists. Our recent world view honored material wealth, freedom from responsibility, deceit, mobility, self-centeredness, and being apart from and outside the laws of nature.

The world-view we need to build on today honors sustainability. To ensure a healthy world, it needs to embrace the needs of the ecological systems that support our lives. It needs to nurture our emotional and spiritual, as well as physical health. And that requires finding a sense of our universe that gives meaning to our lives. It needs to ensure the health of our relationships - with our selves, with each other, and with the rest of Creation. And it needs a deep understanding of our universe and the on-going Creation of which we are part. It needs, in sum, to find a future worth living for.

That world-view is already shaping surroundings far different from our present ones.

Stone bridge
Imperial Palace Garden
Kyoto, Japan

Entry garden
Portland, Oregon

29

3

CHANGE IS INHERENT
IN ALL THINGS

Surf Geyser. Hawaii

Mayan vision serpent representing access to the spirit world achieved during public ritual through the realms of chi energy.

Our culture is embarked on a quiet, yet fundamental change, acknowledging the existence and importance of chi, or life force energy. In November, 1997, the National Institutes of Health released a strong endorsement of the use of acupuncture, noting "very clear-cut evidence" of its successful action and that it is less invasive, and with fewer side effects than conventional treatments.

For a major governmental player in the US medical establishment to make such an endorsement of a practice based on *chi* is remarkable - particularly with the panel noting "there is no evidence that confirms this theory". What is perhaps most remarkable is that in endorsing something denied by our conventional scientific concepts, they are challenging the adequacy of those very concepts! The *chi* underlying acupuncture is the same *chi* in the earth which is central to arts, such as Chinese *feng-shui,* used for aligning ourselves with the energetics of place.

Nature, the British equivalent of *Scientific American*, announced in their December, 1997 issue the successful experimental demonstration of "quantum teleportation" by researchers in Austria. Quantum teleportation shows that information even on the subatomic level is transmitted *instantly* over stellar distances (without being limited by the speed of light). With this demonstration, the informational interconnectedness of all Creation is no longer in question. Related work is underway by IBM.

1997 also witnessed the publication of Dean Radin's *THE CONSCIOUS UNIVERSE*, a publication of previously classified military-funded experimentation on psi phenomena and statistical analysis of experimentation done over the last century in that area. Radin's work should erase any lingering doubts that there is more going on in our universe than meets the rational eye.

"Energy healing", "laying on of hands", and related practices of healing energy work with bodily *chi* has been effective enough in promoting healing in a variety of situations that it is now covered by many health insurance policies. Millions of people in our own culture have also now *experienced* chi energy. It is no longer a theoretical philosophical concept of foreign spiritual traditions. Body work techniques have been developed which make work with *chi* something that can be easily attained by most people. *Chi* is no longer an esoteric practice requiring years of monastic training. Even the US Marines are now using Akido training based on chi!

Our sciences have been so absorbed in the years since World War II in exploring the material consequences of breakthroughs achieved in a few branches of physics that they have neglected to focus their powerful tools on other areas which we unwittingly still relate to with "black box" concepts. Do we really understand something like magnetism? How *does* it transmit power through space and vacuum?

31

Or what about *gravity*? Look up at the Moon tonight. Its mass is immense. Simple mechanics tells us what incredible forces gravity applies to the Moon to keep that mass in orbit and from shooting off on a tangent into space. But how does it work? How are the moon and sun able through enormous distances to *pull* the entire oceans of our planet six feet into the air twice a day, and pull the Earth itself around in a circle? We give names - like gravity or magnetism - to blank spaces in our understanding, but then assume we therefore know more about them than we do.

Chi is part of these areas still unexplored by our current sciences. Unlike the moon visibly hanging over our heads, it has until recently been an area we could brush aside and pretend didn't exist. But experience and success in its use are today forcing its recognition.

It may seem that *chi* is a simple and peripheral thing, but it has been central to the sophisticated philosophies of many cultures. The power inherent in its ac-

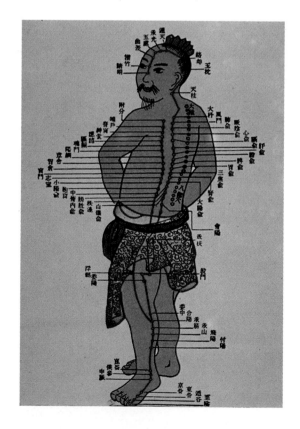

Acupuncture points and meridians on the body channel chi energy. "Knots" of energy form at acupuncture points related to imbalance and incipient illness.

knowledgment is likely to be as foreign and initially inconceivable as the atom bomb was as the outcome of theoretical scratchings of Einstein. Fortunately, the power of chi is an integrative, rather than a destructive one; a power of giving life, rather than of taking it. Its acknowledgment will bring changes - in far different directions - as great as those achieved by our modern technology.

Chi is intimately connected with and inherent in place and our associations with it. Every culture has emphasized and developed certain aspects of place energy, while virtually ignoring others. Feng shui demonstrates various approaches to environmental modification for improving local chi patterns. It has made extensive use of astrological information in siting, and generated culturally-specific practices for aligning our places with *chi* of place.

The European geomantic tradition has developed the mapping of energy flows and concentrations in the earth, and has also located buildings relative to that energy. The Australian Aboriginal tradition has developed use of such energy lines in the earth even further, using them for long distance communication.

Relative to the built environment, the Japanese have developed the role of *li* or intention to great refinement and power. *Chi* (or *ki* in Japanese) is, if anything, more central to Japanese culture and design than to Chinese. The Japanese language, for example, has over 600 terms employing the ideogram for *ki*, compared to about 80 in Chinese, and the concept is central to all of their arts and sciences.

Contemporary work in our own culture by architects and designers working with chi has not reached the refinement of the Japanese or Chinese, but is developing a tradition specific to our own conditions and time. The Khmer culture in Cambodia can show us immensely

The chakras, or centers of chi energy in the body, represented in a variety of cultures, relate to different aspects of our psyches and control different aspects of energetic connection with others.

powerful roles that our built environment can play in connecting us with energy from the spirit world. The Yoruba in Africa can show the emotional power that can be developed afresh in our building drawing directly upon intimate connection with that world.

Many cultures, from the !Kung to the Yoruba and the Dagara in Africa to the Wiccan tradition in Europe, have worked powerfully with community raising of energy, and the roles it holds in cultural survival and health. The recent work of dowsers and energy workers such as Joey Korn, Sig Lonegren and others has shown that earth energies are not immutable. They move and change. We can ask the balancing of negative energies, the focusing and relocation of positive ones. We can call upon them, and they respond - it would appear almost consciously - to our requests for aligning with our lives and activities.

Energetics of place also involves information and communication. Afri-

33

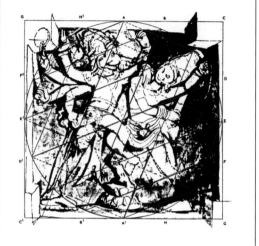

Sculpture in the Kailasa Temple at Ellora, India, is designed on geometric principles related to energetic structure in our bodies, to aid in meditation on different chakras.

can cultures have worked strongly with personal interaction with energy of place to access ancestors and other beings in the realms of energy. Native American, Aboriginal, Celtic, Greek, and many other traditions work with direct communication with, and through, the individual elements of nature. The Australian Aboriginal tradition has developed to a high level use of the unique and specific connections to the spiritual realm from different natural sites. The Khmers and Egyptians have demonstrated how buildings can enhance such connections.

The experience of other cultures with chi is important to us. We are *all* exposed today to all the different traditions of millennia of different cultures' experience. Today is a time of gathering in of the wisdom of all ages. All have things to offer, all have limitations and omissions. It is important to see what any and all can offer to each

other and to how we relate to our surroundings.

Chi or life force communication may be one of the important missing links in our reconnection with nature. Alienation arises from our blocking out the eternal sharing and connection with all life which occurs on that level. As Malidoma Somé has said, literacy may fill a place in our psyches intended for other purposes. But techniques are available for us to set literacy aside when needed, and reestablish direct linkage on the level of *chi.*

These are only a few examples that stand out, for their special developments, from the almost universal use of chi in cultures worldwide. What is exciting is that these are living traditions which can be learned from, shared, melded, and forged into a living tradition for our own culture.

Design, in a *chi*-based world, is a very different animal.

We are discovering that the energy bodies of our communities can be damaged by place-rape and abuse from greed-based activities such as overlogging, overfishing, extractive agriculture, energy and material mining just as our human energy bodies are damaged by rape and abuse. And we've found that healing those energy bodies is possible and essential in both cases for true healing.

We're learning how the *chi* of place and people interact; how our love or anger remains in a place to affect the next users; how gifts of honor and pilgrimage are bestowed on both a place and its subsequent visitors. We're learning how to generate and direct group energy to sustain the joy and health of our human communities and the natural communities within which they live. The

THESE ARE A FEW OF THE QUESTIONS THAT ARISE
WHEN WE ACKNOWLEDGE THE CENTRAL ROLE OF CHI IN OUR UNIVERSE.

• *What are the implications of a world where noone can lie - where our innermost thoughts and feelings are known to each other?*

• *What changes in our lives and society when we acknowledge that instant communication occurs - not only between people, but among all forms of life - stars, rocks, the cells in our bodies?*

• *What does it mean to our society to acknowledge that we continue to exist on an energy level after "death"?*

• *What are the implications of being able to call on the counsel of ancestors and other beings in the spiritual planes of life?*

• *What happens when we discover that astrology can show what kinds of surroundings are good or bad for us at different times?*

• *What happens when we realize that "magic" is practiced and can have powerful effect for good or ill?*

• *How does our culture change when we are all indelibly aware that the health of all Creation is essential to our well-being?*

• *How do we change when we recognize that our minds and hearts are an integral and powerful part of our interaction with the world on both sides of our skin, and that those parts of our existence are inseparable?*

• *What happens when we realize that sacredness is the central basis of meaningful lives and an enduring society?*

Birthing stones in Hawaii are located on nodes of healing energy in the earth.

potentialities for people working with earth energies are expanding in scope, depth, and concrete application.

A *chi*-centered world changes how we design and use places. It first of all requires that we give consideration to the energetic aspects of a place. It means that the kinds of institutions and the kinds of personal needs we design for will be different. It demands integrity of materials, design and uses. It stresses the importance of paying attention to how we feel about a place, the psychology of place, the role of our minds and our fears and dreams. It requires we design relative to the needs and aspirations of all Creation, not just us. Our attitudes and values, what we want in a place, change dramatically.

The exteriors of these Hindu temples represent in sculpture and ornament the diverse richness of the unfolding of Creation. They act also as a process of sacred work and as an offering demonstrating the importance of the sacred in the life of the community. Builders of classical Indian temples constructed yantras in the buildings as part of a ritual to clarify and exhibit their intention and a way of imbuing the building with sacredness.

Matangesuara Temple
Khajuraho, India

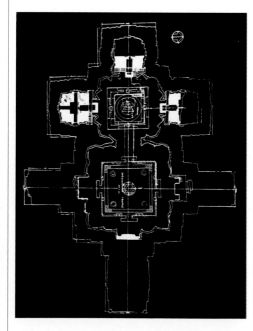

With *chi*, our *intention* in approaching design is critical. An approach that just considers "job functions" delegates people to "back-room" jobs and "back-room" consideration by others, while an intention to provide rewarding jobs changes building configuration and the respect given to each person in their work.

The role of the sacred becomes central. Buildings with soul, gardens for our spirits, cities of passion become the goal rather than rentable square feet. Accommodating and enhancing ritual and its role in both the making and use of places becomes important, as does being a part of the local ecological community. Low-impact ecological design is taken for granted. Growth, greed, and consumption give way to the goals of sustainability and nurture.

In our current time of gathering in, it is vital to open ourselves to the varieties of wisdom of all traditions and glean from each what can be melded together to bear on our unique situations. Chi-energy, or the energetics of place, is a cluster of concepts and tools that can help us begin to find ways to walk in this new world.

Chi, and the connection and wholeness with which it imbues our lives, underlies the spirit of place. The means to access and nurture it show us the place of spirit in our lives and our surroundings.

Images, temples, and other objects and places, can be imbued with chi energy to give linkage to specific entities in the spirit world. This image, of the god Horus (represented by the falcon) speaking through Egyptian Pharaoh Chephren shows the stiff posture frequent to trance-channeling.

THE THREE "I"'S

4

The "nimbus" or halo,
and the glow seen here radiating
from Christ's hands and heart
are expressions of chi often seen also
in liturgical paintings and mosaics
of other traditions.

Chapel, Monmartre
Paris, France

Working with chi and the sacred in our surroundings is connected with, but distinctly different from working with our inner chi for health and in meditation. Meditation processes in most spiritual traditions focus on going inward, cutting off from the outer world, and seeking personal nurture from an inner source.

In contrast, work with chi in our surroundings focuses on opening outward to, connecting with rather than shutting off from, other life. It focuses on using our intention as a basis of action and interaction with others and with place rather than just personal growth. In doing so it reconnects us with the rest of our universe. Simultaneously, it informs all life of our intentions, and allows it to work with us in concert to achieve those intentions.

We can have wonderful inner thoughts and feelings. But until we focus those outward into action, nothing is manifested either in ourselves or in the world around us.

There are three main principles to working with chi in the world outside our skins - chi, li, and tummi. Understanding them prepares us to look in the following chapters at specific tools for action.

CHI - Life Force Energy

Chi is the fuel, intention the blueprint, of energetics of place. Combined with intention, chi forms the subtle energy template upon which our material world takes shape in its many wonderful variations. Health and disease, change and constancy, manifest from the realm of chi into the realm of matter. Chi is vital to supporting our physical as well as emotional and spiritual health. It forms the glue which keeps a community healthy. It is blocked by emotional barriers, artificial building materials, intensive use of electromagnetic devices, and cultural practices based on taking from others.

The pattern and juxtaposition of earth forms, waterways, and materials within the earth's mantle result in places that concentrate or disperse the natural chi of place and similarly affect the chi of inhabitants of those places. In addition to locating good and avoiding bad natural power spots of chi to locate our buildings on, chi energy can be called in, enhanced and worked with by individual intention and group ritual. As connections with the spirit world are located in the realms of chi, places can be made specifically to work with individual and community chi and to act as access points to the spirit world.

As we use and shape places from our hearts, with love, they transform our surroundings into ones which fill our hearts with joy, rightness, and meaning. They reach out and make us again at home in a wonderful world of which we are an integral part.

◄ *Burning of the Sun God at a Midsummer's Night celebration in Cobenhaven, Denmark. Community ritual tied to the changes of season and its effects on our energy are as ancient as the beginnings of time.*

Catscans of dowsers' and healers' heads show unique brain activity patterns in "trance" state.

Dowser Brainwave Study
American Society of Dowsers

Bringing our chi into resonance and harmony with that of a particular locale helps us create moving places of deep harmony.

White House
Canyon de Chelly, Arizona

41

LI - Intention

The second of the three most important aspects of energetics of place is *intention*. *Li, hara,* or intention focuses energy to attain life's purposes. All of our surroundings reflect back to us the intention that has gone into their making and use - the values of their makers. If made from greed, if made to deceive, they convey that. If they come from a meanness of soul or smallness of spirit, they surround us with that essence. If made with love, with generosity, with honoring of all life, they support and evoke the same intentions in our own lives.

Clarity, strength, and rightness of intention also bring life force energy, or chi, into a place, with its ability to nurture our lives. The nature of our intention - whether in making or using a place - reflects that same energy back into our own lives, enhancing or weakening our own energy.

There can be many different levels to our intention. A builder may express an intention to build a good house for someone, but a deeper intention to make a lot of money may alter what results. A person may say they want to build a place with a soul. But deeper values of greed and deceit may lead them to believe that surface appearances are enough, that deeper things don't really matter, and that they can spend their resources on the empty shells of many things rather than one done well which can give true satisfaction. Clarity of intention requires that we carefully examine our core values, and alter them to ones supporting love and life.

Urban advertising
Minneapolis, Minnesota

◀ Whether we wish or not, our surroundings reflect back to us where our deepest personal and cultural values lie.

▶ The intentions surrounding us are so much a part of our lives that we are often unaware of them until we lose them. The wonderful tree-shaded streets of fifty years ago in Midwestern towns didn't just happen, but were created from the intention and efforts of our ancestors.

Elm trees
Buffalo, New York

42

Focused attention to each act in building gives opportunity
to intensify our connection with the materials, the site, our work,
and the spirits of the place.
Finely honed attention and intention involved in construction can
result in a structure where every post, every board, every joint
resonates with the power of the sacred.

Storehouse
Naiku Shrine
Ise, Japan

▲ The Zen tradition in Japan has taken
the art of intention to perhaps greater
heights than any other culture. With that
purity of intent, a single brush stroke
faultlessly conveys the full intention of
the artist.   Crow on Pines, by Niten

43

INTENTION CHANGES LIVES

Our intention towards a place can totally change the lives of others.

Out of an intention of making a Head Start Center good for the kids using it, we once asked what would be most wonderful to us as a kid coming in the door. "The smell of good food!" was the unanimous response. This lead us to put the kitchen right in the middle of the building, open to the classrooms and entry. It worked wonderfully, giving parents a place to stop for a cup of coffee and a chat, and to peek around the corner to know their kids were doing okay. It allowed the cook to be an extra friend and source of snacks and hugs for the kids, and a backup pair of eyes for the teachers.

What we didn't realize until later, was how much our intention totally changed working as a cook in this place. Cooking is usually a "back-room" job, tucked away out of sight in service areas near the loading dock. In contrast, putting the cook in the *middle* of everything, and in contact with everyone, made them a central part of what went on. The design which embodied our intention towards the cook's job would change the life of every person who would ever work as a cook in that place.

An architect later asked what we would do if the center was larger and needed a bigger kitchen and loading dock. I looked at him a minute and said, "You've just defined *'too big'*!" Our gut feeling of 'too big' is really connected with a change in intention - from whole-person, meaningful work to mechanical function being dominant.

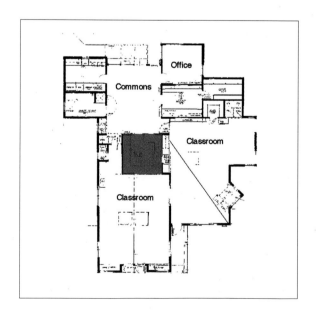

There is nothing special about this Head Start Center kitchen, other than its scale, the intention behind placing it in the center of things, and opening it to the kids, parents and staff of the center. But those decisions transform how the kitchen affects the life of all connected with the Center.

Head Start Center
Seaside, Oregon

45

Benares, India

◀ *If we are disturbed by something from our surroundings or elsewhere, it colors all of our perceptions and actions. If we have reason to feel good about our surroundings or other things, we radiate positive energy to others, into our actions, and into our surroundings.*

TUMMI -
Heeding Our Hearts and Minds

The last of the three main principles of energetics of place deals with the immense importance our minds and hearts play in our energetic relationship with our surroundings. The psychological, emotional, and spiritual aspects of our relationship with place are complex and beautiful, but virtually ignored in our design and use of place. Their complexity means it is often most effective to ignore the details of their interaction and instead to pay attention directly to the end result – how our tummies feel. Our "gut" feelings *are* important, and reflect manifold cultural and personal beliefs. It's important to listen to, and *trust your tummy.*

The expected sitting position of family members and guests in a tipi, a Japanese room, or the home of a French count are utterly different. If a Chinese family *believes* they or someone else has the most favorable feng-shui site, that belief will strongly influence their happiness and success regardless of the actual feng-shui. It probably doesn't matter if you sleep with your feet towards the door, unless your culture has a practice of taking a corpse out of a room feet first and believes you shouldn't sleep that way.

Acknowledging the importance of our gut feelings affirms us, and achieves a degree of success merely in paying attention to and acknowledging the importance of people and their feelings. The importance of our minds and hearts means that many successful chi-related actions don't deal directly with the chi of place but with helping us feel good so we open our hearts and let our energy influence the energy of the place. This energetic level of effect also accounts for the unexpected success of many psychological actions.

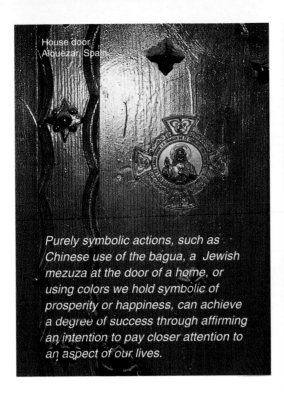

House door
Aiquezar, Spain

Purely symbolic actions, such as
Chinese use of the bagua, a Jewish
mezuza at the door of a home, or
using colors we hold symbolic of
prosperity or happiness, can achieve
a degree of success through affirming
an intention to pay closer attention to
an aspect of our lives.

▼ There are often subtle clues that warn our
tummies of real but not immediate hazards.
There are energetic issues with living at the
end of a "t" intersection, but there are also
distractions from headlights and noise, and
the real potential of a vehicle failing to turn
the corner in hazardous conditions.

Manzanita, Oregon

Sometimes we are unable to alter things in our surroundings that bother us. It
may still be possible to take advantage of the importance of our minds
to our comfort and give them something positive to associate with
which can counter the negative energy.

The Chinese might hang a flute on a heavy beam
they feel pressing down on them
to counter that energy
with the lightness associated with music.
Native Americans might hang a feather below the beam.

Even our culture has its talismans
that can lighten our minds.

Neahka

ELEMENTS
OF
ENERGETICS OF PLACE

Energetics of place is concerned with the relationships between our personal chi energy and the chi energy in places. It calls our attention to the cycles of change in energy that move through both nature and our own lives, and suggests ways to bring our lives in harmony with those changes. It helps us find nurture in natural places and to make and use our own homes and work places so they also sustain our lives and the rest of Creation. It shows how clear intention, giving welcome, honoring others, making places that have a soul, or bringing our ancestors and the spirit world into our everyday life can give richness and meaning to both our places and our lives.

With the diversity and unfamiliarity of chi-related actions possible from various traditions, it is important to understand the relative significance and effectiveness of the different elements. Different situations have different needs. Different individuals and communities have different skills and traditions. Most people don't know a Nine Star Ki from a Yellow River Chart. But they may very well know whether they need the clearing of a space from old chi, a balancing or enhancing of existing earth energy, or a gateway for them to connect with their ancestors in the spirit world.

48

▶ *Natural places with powerful chi open our hearts to resonate and connect with the bountiful nature of all life.*

What follows is *my own* list of elements and my sense of their relative significance, *today*. Every one of us will have our own, different, list. *All* will change as we understand these elements more deeply. And all these elements interact with and affect each other. Our energy is best put where we sense it will be most effective, and different situations benefit best from different actions.

Coast Redwoods, California

49

ELEMENTS OF ENERGETICS OF PLACE

ELEMENT and Importance	ITS NATURE	ACTIONS	DURATION
1 *MOVING BEYOND A GREED-CENTERED CULTURE*	Beside this, all other actions pale. Damage to our body and home energetics from TV is far greater than energetic "cures" can heal. Similarly massive are the negative impacts on our essential self-esteem and mutual respect which emerge from institutional work patterns. Tourism injects cultural values of "taking" into our connection to people and place.	* *Participatory rather than passive recreation and entertainment* * *Work, learning, family, and institutional patterns that support our sense of doing valued work, contributing to our community, and acknowledging our worth* * *All actions affirming a love- and life-centered world improve our nurture*	Finding alternatives to cultural values and patterns such as TV, tourism, and bureaucratic work patterns may offer the greatest and most enduring energetic benefit of any actions we can take.
2 *DIRECT RAISING AND NURTURE OF CHI*	Direct raising and nurture of chi is far more vital for community health than even for our individual health. It is a practice almost totally neglected today.	* *Group spiritual practice* * *Community ritual and energy raising* * *Cathartic conflict resolution* * *Internal or external chi adjustments, blessings* * *Use of mantras, mudras, yantras and visualization* * *Simple actions by individuals and communities involving love and giving, and transference to a society based on care and mutual respect may be as productive as community ritual or "shamanic" practices*	Sustaining direct raising of community chi is an on-going process. Repetition builds long-lasting patterns.
3 *THE PERSONAL ENERGY OF USERS*	Our energy flows are, with few exceptions, the largest energy flows in our homes and communities.	* *Individual spiritual practice* * *Actions which enhance our emotional health, self-esteem or sense of being of value to our community* * *Practices which open us to deeper energetic flows in our surroundings* * *Places which bring shelter, nurture, challenge, and harmony to our lives* * *Symbolic actions affecting our emotional and mental interfaces with our surroundings*	Successful individual changes can last a lifetime. Symbolic actions rarely survive the tenancy of a single user of a place or have the power of actions that actually alter underlying patterns.

ELEMENT and Importance	ITS NATURE	ACTIONS	DURATION
4 *GOOD* *NATURAL* *CHI* *IN* *LAND* *AND* *PLACE*	Finding, enhancing, and creating resonance with natural flows and patterns of chi in place - not for advantage over others, but to communicate and interact more fully - is a wonderful source of sustenance. Some chi of place comes from topography, some from geophysical anomalies, some from how we have attuned the places we build to channel and enhance those energies.	* *"Tangible" feng shui practices - forms and compass school, adjustments relative to interior and exterior factors such as roads, trees, hillsides or waterways, location of doors, beds, bathrooms or workplaces* * *Dowsing to locate and move chi* * *Calling in of energy balancing and enhancement* * *Design of homes, gardens, and communities to focus and sustain place energy*	Good natural chi in land and place may endure for millennia, or change tomorrow due to new road cuts, underground water movement, dams, power lines, ground water withdrawal, etc. Requires monitoring to verify continuation.
5 *ATTENTION* *TO* *INTENTION* *(LI)*	Intention, purpose, and its expression in the soul of a place *can* be the most accessible way to change the energy of a place and its users.	* *Consensus on placemaking goals and their alignment with goals of the rest of Creation* * *Clarity in the specifics of our actions, with those goals as touchstone* * *"Hara"-based practices of individual action and group decision-making* * *Ritual in the building process* * *Attitudes towards work, materials, and the spirit world*	Intention can rapidly change energy of a place, but it can be countered by intention of others or existing energy patterns. Deep intention embodied with physical actions gives greatest impact and duration.
6 *DESIGN -* *HARMONY* *OF* *INNER* *ATTRIBUTES* *AND* *PATTERNS* *OF* *PLACE*	Real harmony comes from intention and from right relationship of attributes and inner patterns. This is very much the opposite of conventional design that focuses on outward appearances.	* *Creating place as invisible servants* * *Tying to the cycles of nature* * *Honoring* * *Gardens to nurture our spirits* * *Connecting to our community in nature* * *Eliminating mirrors* * *Celebrating night, rain, and death* * *Durability* * *Building through rewarding work* * *Putting love, giving, and silence into the places we make*	Design changes may last as long as the facility, or be negated by other changes or use patterns.

ELEMENT and Importance	ITS NATURE	ACTIONS	DURATION
7 *RELATION TO ANCESTORS AND THE SPIRIT WORLD*	Wholeness requires we reopen the doors to our ancestors, to the spirits, and to the non-material worlds - to honor, and work together to manifest the great unfolding of Creation.	* Establishing temples, shrines, home alters, and sacred places * Learning design of "gateways" to the spirit world * Rituals and places maintaining ongoing connection between the material and spirit world * Design and placement of tombs as in traditional feng shui, scattering of ashes, honoring of ancestors	Acknowledging and restoring connection to the spirit world can result in long-enduring energy shifts. Individual actions may have varied impacts.
8 *CLEARING, CLEANSING, AND CLUTTER*	This element involves simplifying, focusing intention and energy, and eliminating extraneous diversions. It is often a prefatory action of clearing intention prior to direct raising of chi, enhancing the energy of individual users, or specific practices and rules. In our materialistic lives, it is valuable for letting go of the past, or to consider in itself.	* Dealing with the inheritance of good or bad chi from prior use of a place such as death, bankruptcy, anger, divorce, or illness * Internal clearing such as fasting, meditation, or Zen training * External purification, dealing with accumulated material "stuff", cleaning, and honoring * Balancing, freeing or relocating bad chi and li; exorcism of ghosts	Dealing with clutter may last minutes or years, depending on how deeply inner patterns are changed. Internal clearing can give life-long change. Clearing inherited chi of a place can have long-enduring results.
9 *SPECIFIC PRACTICES AND RULES*	Attending to specific real-world psychological, cultural, and ecological problems of people and place is as important and effective as a grand theoretical approach to a situation.	* Taking care of lighting, sanitation, ventilation, structural adequacy, and setting needed for rituals * Traditional feng shui practices such as classic "T" intersections, heavy beams, or bad bed locations * Verifying applicability of "rules" by "following your tummy" - paying attention to what feels right	Varies with individual situations and actions.

ELEMENT and Importance	ITS NATURE	ACTIONS	DURATION
10 *ALIGNING WITH THE COSMOS*	This includes symbolism embodying philosophical, social, and cosmological principles; astrology, numerology, five elements, and the feng shui bagua. Beyond any direct connections, aligning with the cosmos also strengthens our will and sense of the rightness of our beliefs and actions. Major significance, very different from existing beliefs and practices, may await discovery here.	* *Symbolism in house or city design* * *Astrology of place takes two main forms - a) birth-influenced desires and needs for surroundings (Chinese Nine Star Ki); and b) time-specific compatibility with places depending upon position in our personal time cycles (Chinese Eight Words or Four Pillars)* * *The Elements (Earth, Air, Water, Fire, and Metal in Chinese tradition) alert us to the qualities of change cycles, particularly chi-related, to which we must relate* * *Traditions of cosmic connection from different cultures for elements of homes, villages, and ritual*	Individual birth needs are lifelong. Position in time cycles change periodically. Symbolism in design and layout has impact as long as aligned with beliefs of society and affirmed in fresh and clear ways.
11 *OUTWARD APPEARANCE (HSING)*	Harmony, beauty, and balancing *yin* and *yang* in how things look are only "fine-tuning". Yet outer appearances *do* affect us and our perception of meaning. And through them we can also see what inner intentions are being manifested.	* *Fine-tuning the esthetics, the physical expression, and the patterns of a place to enrich its ability to resonate with our hearts and our lives.* * *Maintaining inner intention as a touchstone so as to not fabricate appearances at odds with what lies within*	Affected by rate of change in society and how much "fashions" change our sense of beauty or harmony. The best work has enduring value. The worst loses value immediately.
12 *OTHER...?*	Every situation provides unique avenues of action which resist codification. Look for what other elements might be apply and be important in your individual case.	* *Varies with situation*	Duration varies with individual situation and action.

RIGHT DURATION

In addition to the initial effectiveness of an action, we need equally to consider the *duration* of its impact. Duration is an aspect of place energetics rarely given proper attention. Some actions are long-lasting, some need frequent repetition. Long-lasting chi-influencing actions need periodic monitoring, and short-lasting ones need repetition. Actions affecting us, rather than our places directly, may need to change when users of a place change. So it is important to be clear about *all* that is required to sustain good chi in our relations with place over time, and to choose from the widening range of possible actions ones which best assist us in reaching that goal.

Right duration is an important consideration in all we do. Because it is loved, a building with a soul may often endure beyond the needs of its makers to become a gift to future generations. A cathedral lasting twenty generations, or a bridge lasting twenty centuries can give back far more than the effort put in their making. Such endurance immeasurably alters the per-generation cost of resources and work gone into creating our communities. *Durability thus grants a generosity to the places we make that can be obtained in few other ways.*

A building with a soul would be as comfortable a thousand years in the past or future as it is today. It is comfortable with the changes of time, neglect, and love - mellowing and becoming enriched rather than tarnished and tattered. There is a hoary strength and a nourishing peacefulness in the timeless qualities of a building that truly fits our hearts and spirits.

Yet everything does not benefit from lasting longer than its nature. A generation from now we may wish that *some* of the things that we have recently created had not lasted beyond their time and intention. It may be good that our homes or vehicles are durable. It may not be desirable that our foods or some of our building materials are preserved with poisons that linger and harm.

Stone Beam Bridge
Fukien Prov., China

◀ *Single slabs of granite spanning 80 to 90 feet. Immense skill and understanding of material. Over a thousand years or so, the cost of this bridge has been repaid again and again and again. It represents a far different economic calculus than what we employ.*

In India, walking along a single country road we can be surrounded by the ghosts and ruins of untold centuries and dynasties of building. A builder or an artist might be inspired by the accumulations of centuries of the greatest achievements of their society. Or they might find those achievements too lofty a yardstick against which to have their own work measured and not even begin to discover what they themselves could create anew. Things that endure can be both a gift and a burden.

It is good, therefore, that some things last and that some things do not persist, making room for each generation and individual to forge anew the understandings and relationships of a meaningful life. The Inuit who throws away a scrimshaw carving once the empowering act of creation is finished, or the Balinese village or Indian pueblo that returns imperceptibly to the earth when its use is finished holds a rightness of duration and of material choice.

Finding the right duration for each of our creations is one of the roots of wisdom needed for being a true part of the ever-evolving creation of life.

What does duration feel like?
How much is a path worn away
by 300 generations of footsteps?
How deeply do we look at the framework
of our actions in time?

Loess road, China

55

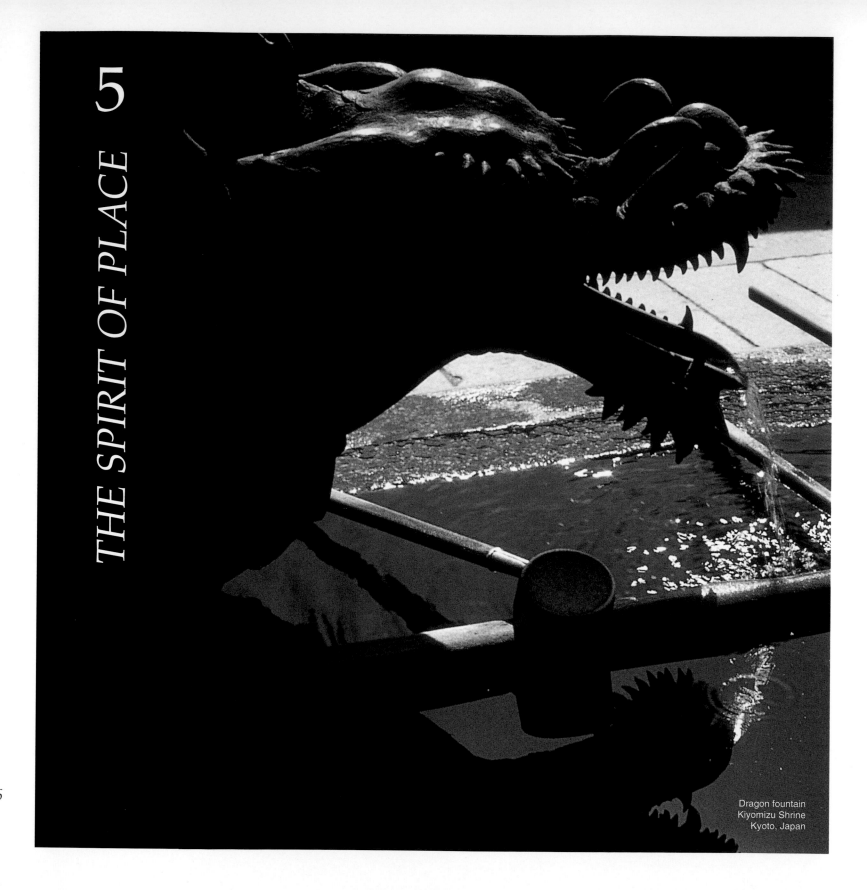

THE SPIRIT OF PLACE   5

Dragon fountain
Kiyomizu Shrine
Kyoto, Japan

56

*O*ne obvious way of working with subtle energy and the sacred in our surroundings is to directly alter the chi energy - either individually or in concert with others. This involves centering, grounding, opening our chakras, establishing connections from them to other people, other life about us, or other dimensions of life. We can then work with our intention to achieve what we seek to affect.

But the chi-based dimension of our lives is also deeply interwoven with, and interacts with, our more familiar material dimensions. Actions we can take in our everyday lives can affect and direct events on the chi level, often more easily than actions on the chi dimension itself. Simply having new insight into the value of something in our lives, or the of how things operate and interact, can change our actions and their energetic consequences with little further effort needed. What is involved, in part, is realigning our sense of our selves and how we are part of a larger organism.

The following four chapters give a brief introduction with examples from our own and other cultures to some of the more important concepts we can use to affect the energy of our surroundings. Trying some, we can see if things begin to feel different.

Ocean beach
Neahkahnie. Oregon

NATURAL
PLACES OF
POWER

Spring maples
Kiyomizu Temple
Kyoto, Japan

We can feel the power of chi energy where the primal forces of nature come together in intense and memorable relationships. In such natural places of power our hearts are moved, our spirits made full, our dreams become more powerful and our lives are reaffirmed.

Such places have been sought from time immemorial for inspiration, for healing, for guidance, and for the pure celebration of their wonder. Some contain intense chi energy in themselves and encompass us and nurture us with that energy. Others, through the intense beauty of their nature, move our hearts and awaken the chi within us.

Some are places of immense power, physical size, and energy - volcanoes, crashing surf, roaring waterfalls, wild winds, towering trees, grand vistas. Others are still and intimate, deep in their energy - the beauty of a flower, a drop of water on a blade of grass, the silence of a desert night or of falling snow.

Some such places are exotic and foreign to us and we come to them with fresh eyes and astonished hearts. Others are utterly familiar and inseparable parts of our lives - our natures becoming more entwined and inseparable every day.

Allowing the energy of such places to open our hearts, fill us, and connect us with the power of nature can give us an inner touchstone of peace, connectedness and nurture. That touchstone can help us achieve rightness in our everyday lives and actions.

Wall Street
Bryce Canyon NP, Utah

59

HUMAN PLACES OF POWER

The breath of life, or CHI, pervades all people, places, and things; and is vital to their interaction. Chi accumulates in places from acts of commitment, care and honoring. Human places of power have developed where inspired construction has focused and augmented natural places of energy on the site. It also collects where historical events or deeply motivated building has resulted in places that profoundly affect us. In those places, the resulting intensity of human emotion accumulates human energy, which then draws to it the chi energy of the earth.

This power of nature can be consciously called into focus, balance and harmony in our places and our lives. We can ask directly that the powers of nature converge to bring into balance any detrimental energies and to enhance the beneficial energies of the place for those who use it and for all life, for now and into the future for as long as is appropriate.

The Chess Pavilion on HuaShan in China places our lives in context with the powers of Creation.

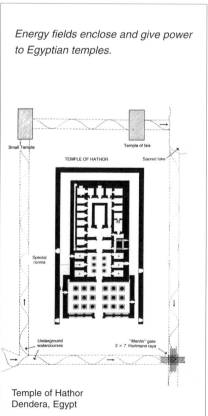

Energy fields enclose and give power to Egyptian temples.

Temple of Hathor
Dendera, Egypt

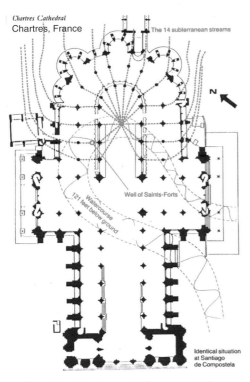

Chartres Cathedral
Chartres, France

The 14 subterranean streams

N

Watercourse 121 feet below ground

Well of Saints-Forts

Identical situation
at Santiago
de Compostela

*Churches, temples, and other sacred places
of many cultures, have been consciously
located on power spots through the process
of divination or dowsing.*

*Gifts to place from love deepen and enrich that power.
While tourism takes from a place, pilgrimage
 brings it a gift of valuing, honoring,
 and loving. This accumulates
and strengthens the energy
of the place and what
it in turn can give
to us.*

61

Chapel
S. Germain des Pres
Paris, France

Kiyomizu Temple
Kyoto, Japan

MOVING IN ENERGY

Construction of a classical seven circuit labyrinth. Spacing of the dots and lines set the path width. Making the paths double width, then drawing a line down the middle out from the center, allows unhindered passing when large numbers of people are using the labyrinth together in ritual.

Moving within the energy fields of a place with our hearts open brings our energy into resonance with that of the place, and augments both. This occurs in Sufi dancing, labyrinth walking, pramayana or circumambulation of sacred places, in any sacred procession, and in ecstatic ritual dancing in different cultures. Energy maps of European churches (previous page) also show the traces of the paths and foci of pilgrimage visitors over the centuries.

Model of the stupa of Borobudur in Java showing pilgrims' path.

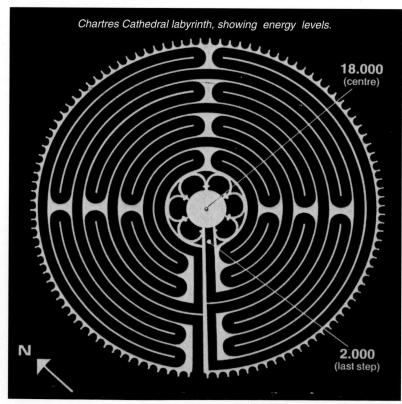

Chartres Cathedral labyrinth, showing energy levels.

18.000
(centre)

2.000
(last step)

N

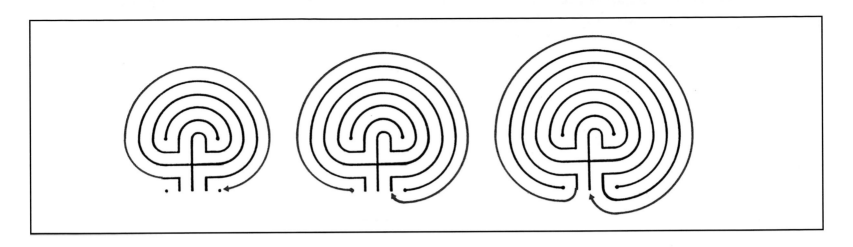

This practice of movement is part of the energetics of sacred places worldwide. Islamic pilgrims circle the kaaba in Mecca. Buddhist and Hindu pilgrims alike circumambulate Kailasanath or Mt. Meru. Christians in the Gothic cathedrals of Europe make their rounds of the shrines in the churches. Visitors to the Buddhist monument of Borobudur in Java circle the monument on each level as they wend their way to the top. In all cases, the energetics of both the place and the pilgrim are accentuated in the process.

Our movement in sacred procession aligns our physical, mental, emotional, and spiritual attention into an act of honoring, opening us into alignment with the energy of place.

Kasuga Shrine
Nara, Japan

63

Newel post
Neahkahnie, Oregon

BUILDINGS

There is life in *all* Creation. There are wombs in space that give birth to galaxies and stars. The hearts of stars sing like bells. The rocks under our feet thrumm with messages from within and around the world. Trees make love with a thousand others at the same time. Microfauna in our cells create communities and transportation systems. Communities have personalities. A forest is a single organism. Planets have consciousness. And they all sing together in harmonious celebration of life.

A place with a soul gives refuge and sanctuary. It fills primal psychic needs - for protection, for warmth, for companionship, for meaning. It helps us marshal our inner resources and stimulates us to use those resources for growth. It affirms sacredness and meaning in our lives and surroundings, and creates places for our hearts and minds as well as our bodies. It draws on and connects us to power extending beyond just the material world.

WITH A SOUL

Places, even, *do* have souls. Small or great, gentle or fierce, nurturing or debilitating. Like all life, distinct and often strong personalities. They have auras, and energy bodies. They are touched and altered by our regard or disregard of them, and they are able to move our hearts and alter our lives. They can enrich, empower, and connect us. In their most powerful form, places connect us into, and allow us to coexist in, the non-material planes of existence as well as the material one. With them, we can individually or as a group expand our conscious presence into some of those other realms.

We have been able to learn in recent years how to create places which do have souls - which give us peace and joy, and which continue to unfold and enrich our lives the more we are part of them. When the pieces are right, all who enter such places breathe a sigh of relief and joy. Their legs get rubbery and they want to just sit and soak in the energy of the place.

The making of such places *is* an act of magic. It involves an intention filled with love, respect and desire for wholeness. It embodies *generosity* - giving rather than taking or paying. It honors its surroundings, materials, users, and the skills gone into its making. It has the coherence of clear vision of the possibilities it can unfold. Flowers, laughter, the smell of fresh bread - these simple things alone can create places with souls that nurture our own.

Home Office
Salem, Oregon

Window seat
Neahkahnie, Oregon

65

Terrace steps
Neahkahnie, Oregon

◄ *Our places are enriched and given meaning through connection with other things. They nestle into and celebrate their unique ecological community which has evolved through the on-going testing of centuries. They touch the spirit of where they are. They bring us into closer touch with each other, the rest of the world and the rhythms of nature.*

▼ *Some places are just for the soul.*

Tea pavilion
Ritsurin Garden
Takamatsu, Japan

Henry Moore sculpture
Tuileries

◄ *A building with a soul is filled with emptiness, and reverberates with the peace of silence. It is free of unnecessary possessions and mechanical noises, and open to the joyful sounds of bird song, laughter, and the sound of the wind. It draws back into shadow, letting the light and attention rest on its inhabitants and their partners in Creation. It has learned restraint and simplicity, and the ability to say, "No."*

▶ *Local materials, ways of building, traditions of design, and patterns of living give a rightness to place. A good place uses local wisdom for dealing with the always unique climate and possibilities of heating, cooling, ventilating and sheltering. Using long-term economics, it ultimately demands fewer resources for its creation, operation and maintenance.*

Kitchen
Neahkahnie, Oregon

67

Toshodaiji
Nara, Japan

*It does not take acres of land
and an army of gardeners
to create a garden of the spirit.
It takes only the will
to honor and embrace the spirit of life.*

GARDENS OF THE SPIRIT

A garden is a curious thing.

We know it is not flowers or plants or water or shade, or the music of birds (though such things are often part of gardens). We know this because we all know wonderful places which are certainly gardens, yet in which some or all of these delightful things are absent.

What a garden really is, is a place we make in our surroundings...*solely for our spirits.*

A garden is a place created and reserved - to give joy, peace, sanctuary, or a sense of connection with worlds other than that of our mundane everyday activities. It is a place, most simply, of *giving*, of that impulse of love which underlies all life and creation. And it is a place where we can recognize, in the reflection of our touch, that we *are* in

▶   Passion, love, paradise. A garden to embrace and evoke all.

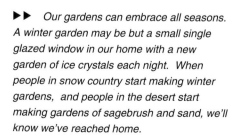

▶▶   Our gardens can embrace all seasons. A winter garden may be but a small single glazed window in our home with a new garden of ice crystals each night. When people in snow country start making winter gardens, and people in the desert start making gardens of sagebrush and sand, we'll know we've reached home.

68

Lake Palace garden
Udaipur, India

Window ice
Minneapolis Minnesota

touch with the heart of the universe which sustains and creates all life.

Gardens connect us with the unique spirit of the diverse places where we live, and with the daily rhythms of the sun, stars, and the seasons. Focusing solely on the needs of our spirits, gardens have a special ability to embody the principles of energetic design. In meditation gardens, they can assist us in connecting directly to the energetic basis of all creation. They can create and enhance energy fields in the Earth's crust, raise our spirits, and enhance our chi.

They can bring us in touch with time and duration beyond our own scope; with death and rebirth, with ancestors and descendants, and with the cosmologies we evolve. They can be a vehicle for expressing sacredness, for honoring and celebrating the multitudinous dimensions of creation.

But most vitally, they can bring our hearts directly in contact with the power of Creation.

Ritsurin Garden
Takamatsu, Japan

Which endures - rock or water? The persistence of water wears away even the hardest rock. A water garden without water. A meditation on power and time.

69

CITIES
OF
PASSION

It is our shared dreams and passions that shape our cities and give them power to move our hearts and affect our lives. Cities, like buildings, have personalities and reflect the way of life of their makers. Cities vivid in our memories are those tied to passions - our own or someone else's. Passions are things that open, build, and focus energy - for an individual, and even more so for a group. A place we value is often one which has developed distinctive and unlikely character out of the quirks, enthusiasms, ardor or zeal, of some individual or group which shaped its nature and its destiny.

What changes city to community is intimacy. A community arises when we share bonds of friendship, history, hardship, or caring. It arises when we open our hearts to share our inner longings, fears, and stories. It arises when we create places of safety where we can speak from the heart, develop compassion about others' needs, and experience the joys of giving. It emerges when we join together our energies with common intention for good.

Taos Pueblo, New Mexico

▲ In cities throughout the world where transport by water is important, a different energy pervades the community. In Venice, Italy, the sound of a Verdi opera fills the canals as a gondolier quietly poles his boat along.

▲ The enchanted Tivoli Gardens in Cobenhaven, Denmark, casts its magic over the hearts of the entire

▲ In pueblo villages, children are taught that they exist as activators for sacred sites within the village. Shrines buried in the ground are pushed into aliveness by their bodies' pressure on them. The resonating vibrations are always changing, so people in the village are always alive with energy.

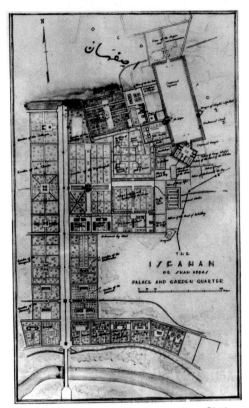

▲ For Persians, paradise is a garden. Shah Abbas' 15th century capital of Isfahan was a city of gardens, flowers, shade, water and music - not buildings.

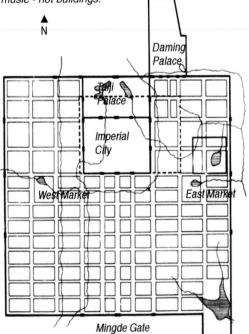

PLAN OF CHANGAN (618-907)

◄ The plan layout of a Chinese capital city surrounds daily life with the principles of place and relationships in the cosmology and the values upon which the culture is based.

▲ Cafes and cathedrals create community in European cities.

71

COMMUNITY AND SPIRIT

6

Ocean beach, Oregon

*T*he *"community" that our lives are played out in is larger than just the people we see around us in our neighborhood. It includes the ecological community of other life,– within which our survival and well-being is entwined differently in each place. It includes the air, water, and the Earth itself. It includes entities and ancestors in the spirit realm, and forces of life in other dimensions of existence.*

The future that we chart gains immensely in power and beauty when we connect through the worlds of chi to the other members of our community and work together - in concert with heaven and earth - to pursue and attain goals that fulfill and enrich all.

HEALING DISEASES OF THE SPIRIT

The truly rampant diseases in our culture are not of the body, but are *diseases of the spirit*. They arise from lack of self-esteem and mutual respect, from not being of value to our community, or not finding meaning in our lives. They reflect an inner shame of taking from others - of living off exploitation of people, places and resources. They grow from the poisons we contain within us when we emotionally wall ourselves off from the pain our actions cause the rest of Creation.

Diseases of the spirit find expression in rape, substance abuse, addictions, violence, crime, obesity, isolation, depression and despair - things possible in any culture, but overpowering in ours. They arise from the root violence in our deepest cultural values.

Healing diseases of the spirit requires that we honor and nurture, not neglect, the emotional and spiritual well-being of all Creation, not just our own. It requires nurturing our souls and opening our hearts - restoring self-esteem and love of others. In our surroundings this requires the honoring of the materials, the elements and forces of nature, the rhythms and cycles of life, the users of a place, and other forms of life.

All things done with reverence restore health, provide nurture, and enhance well-being.

Patitana, India

◄ *The sacred cows of India represent a learning to say "No" to our limitless desires and to acknowledge that the needs of others are a vital part of health.*

74

▶ *Surroundings which express immense skill in their making celebrate the potentials that exist in each of us.*

Ceiling, Dilwarra Temple
Mt. Abu, India

Shrinerock 3
Neahkahnie, Oregon

*It does not take massive constructions or great art
to convey that we hold all life sacred.
A simple marker stone or flag
can keep us aware of the values we honor.*

Community "barn-raising"
Fire Mountain School
Falcon Cove, Oregon

*Joining together in community and
ritual brings cathartic release, heals
us, and forms the glue of enduring
community.*

Christmas decorations
Sunset Highway, Oregon

ANY act of giving brings healing and joy.

75

THE HEALTH OF ALL CREATION

All of Creation makes our lives possible, and gives them meaning and purpose. With more than half of net photosynthesis on our planet going to human uses, we need to significantly change our values and actions to ensure the survival of the natural systems which support us.

Ecological building using renewable resources, efficiency improvement in all parts of our society, and limiting our numbers and appetites are all necessary actions. Moving from self-centeredness to holding inviolate the complex natural world requires also a deep change in our values. Only that can give us context and be a touchstone for right action.

▲ *Honoring other life makes us aware of their wonder, their needs, and their contributions. Finding beauty in the patterns of larval tunnels in wood change them in our minds from a pest to a fellow part of creation.*

▶ *Limiting our demands, numbers, and resource use allows space for the complex dynamics of ecosystems necessary for our own survival and well-being.*

76

Hasadera village
Hasadera, Japan

Cupola, Hasht Behesht
Isfahan, Iran

▶ *The Hasht Behesht garden pavilion is a delightful place to live in Isfahan's desert climate - cool in the summer, warm in the winter. The sun's heat on its masonry dome warms the air inside, which rises out of the building through windows in the cupola at the top of the dome, drawing in cool air from the gardens. In winter, the windows are closed. As the sun's heat radiates through the masonry dome, it warms the air inside . Using natural processes instead of machines can reduce our demands on the rest of Creation.*

▲

Stepping stones
Kyoto, Japan

◀ *A process of co-creation with other nature intelligences through the realm of energetics of place can ensure that the needs of all life are balanced in what we do.*

Hasht Behesht
Isfahan, Iran

GIVING

In a culture rooted in taking from others and keeping things to ourselves, the act of giving is a powerfully transformative deed. Expressed in the shaping and use of our surroundings, it becomes the embodiment of the spirit needed for sustainability as individuals and as a culture. Giving enriches places through what can be provided for other people or other life in the process of building. Trees or flowers to give shade, fragrance, or beauty to adjacent public areas. Pedestrian ways to cut through large projects to connect neighboring areas. Low walls that can be seating. Facilities that can be used by the community when not needed by the primary users. All these are gifts.

Providing habitat for birds, spiders, bats, and butterflies; restoring creeks and watersheds, or providing wildlife migration routes, are all forms of giving. An even more important gift might be restraining our building to allow room for the rest of nature to life unthreatened. A place may well achieve the generosity of spirit central to giving in surprising ways - like a Japanese room, which is generous in space because of its *emptiness*, not because of its size. Generosity is created out of the love and energy put into making. Giving opens the hearts of donor and recipient alike, and allows chi to flow.

▼ *During the dry season in northwest India, village water sources fall to dozens of feet below the surface. A tradition has developed of wealthy landowners giving funds to build access to the water. Shrines are erected at the entrance, and the cool and shady stone galleries become community gathering places.*

▼ *This proposal for a Korean-American Culture Center in Los Angeles, California, made a gift to the community by organizing its plan so that facilities could be used by others after hours.*

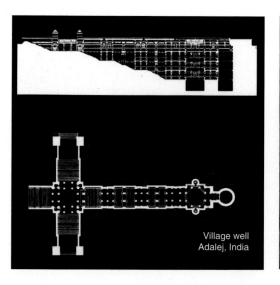

Village well
Adalej, India

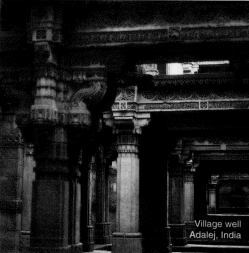

Village well
Adalej, India

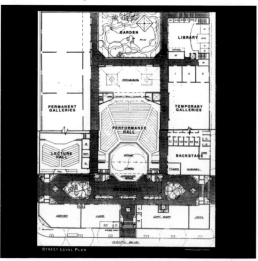

Giving takes many forms.

Trees given to a neighbor create privacy for both, and ensure the neighbor can trim the trees to keep their view.

Privacy tree planting
Neahkahnie, Oregon

Prague, Czech Rep.

▲ *Walking through a city, we are enfolded by a thousand years of gifts of love from residents, artists, and sculptors.*

Durability is a gift to future generations.

◄ *A simple thing like flowers can be a gift of beauty and caring.*

S. Chapelle
Paris, France

79

HONORING

What we know well, we come to love. What we love, we come to know well. These things we come to hold close to our hearts we hold inviolate, protect, and celebrate. Allowing that honoring and celebration to infuse the places we inhabit keeps what we honor in our attention and surrounds us with an atmosphere of love. It enhances self-esteem, mutual respect, and being of value to the rest of life - healing diseases of the spirit. It, also, works even more effectually on the energetic level than on the material one.

Honoring is a giving of respect. A building can honor its surroundings. We can honor the lives of materials which were given up to make its existence possible by allowing their history, beauty, and power to come through their use in ways that move our hearts. In respecting building tradition we honor the insights and wisdom gained by the past. By planting trees, we honor a hope for a future.

▼ *The ways of honoring are many. The Japanese honor a guest by seating them in front of a tokonoma recess containing flowers, art, or calligraphy. Associating the guest with the beauty and power of the art is felt of greater value than the guest being seated to see the art.*

▼ *Honor life, and the power that brings it forth. People and other life are primary, our possessions of less import. Ask those who have escaped tragedy. Seek what truly gives joy. Honor places we hold sacred, the sacredness in ourselves, others, and all that makes our world.*

Tokonoma
Abbot's Residence, Myoshinji
Kyoto, Japan

Lummi Indian with prayer flute
Fudo Shrine, Japan

► *A door handle, made from a root grown squeezed among the pebbles on a beach. Like the wrinkles and stoops of an old person, its gnarled shape tells of the adventures and struggles that have become both its history and its nature. There is power and beauty in both worth sharing and making part of our own lives.*

81

Entry door
Neahkahnie, Oregon

The soul of a place comes from the song of the many lives it contains. Release the rain coming off our roofs from the pipes where we have hidden it away. Celebrate it so its song can join with that of the birds whom we give place to nest, and that of the creatures which feed the birds, and the song of the grasses and trees that breathe our air and give us theirs. The more voices that sing with and around us, the richer the harmony of which our lives are part.

Roof gargoyle
Visitors' Center
Cannon Beach, Oregon

CELEBRATING

The act of celebrating builds and links energy as a joyful giving of thanks. It commemorates birth, age, death, creativity, and this year's harvest. It honors all life, and the power that begets it.

Our surroundings can celebrate our inner resources as well as our material ones. It is amazing the wonderful places that can be created from will, courage, endurance, giving, love, curiosity, passion, joy, wit, wonder, gratitude and forgiveness (to name a few) rather than merely wood and stone.

82

Roof drain
Portland, Oregon

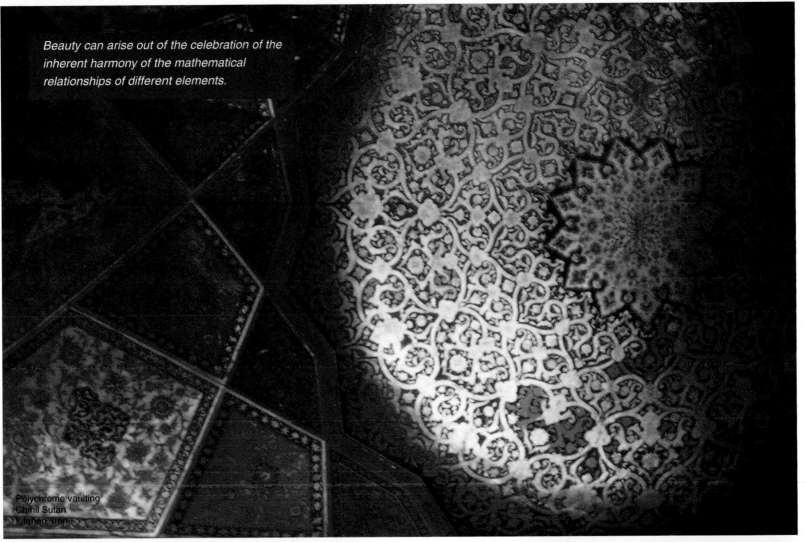

Beauty can arise out of the celebration of the inherent harmony of the mathematical relationships of different elements.

Polychrome vaulting
Chihil Sutan
Isfahan, Iran

Tree table
Lanser Alm, Austria

*Celebration.
Simplicity of execution,
creativity of conception.*

▶ *Celebrate water. The echoing sound and movement of water rushing down beside the steps turns a common stairway into an exhilarating experience of walking down a waterfall.*

Stairs
Kiyomizu Temple
Kyoto, Japan

83

CHANGING COMMUNITY CHI

Community chi is the glue of culture - the result of shared values, beliefs, and energy reflected back to us from our human surroundings. It is the joy or fear we feel walking down a street at night or being approached by a lover or a stranger in the dark. It is the dread or excitement we feel as we enter a school, or hospital, or government building. It is the emptiness or fullness we feel as we leave a church, shrine, or temple. It is the shared meaningfulness or emptiness of our lives which we gain from our surroundings, communities, and culture.

It is not only what our surroundings reflect but what they *don't* reflect which communicates to us our community chi, which creates resonance in our hearts, and which nurtures our personal and community health. Those gaps and silences, those darknesses where nothing is reflected when something *should* be reflected, are possibly the most essential aspects of community chi to be dealt with if we are to create wholeness in our lives and society.

Place-rape happens - the energy bodies of communities and places suffer the same kind of damage that individual auras do from traumatic events. Intentional healing can be performed on the chi of a place or community as well as an individual, to begin restoration of the energy source of the community well-being.

Oko-no-in
Kiyomizu
Kyoto, Japan

▲ *Shrines provide a place for nurture and grounding. They focus and accumulate chi so we can more easily bring our energy into resonance with it, and reinforce the sense of the sacred within us essential for public institutions as well.*

84

▶ *We can, like other cultures, live intimately with other life and open our souls to their special gifts and wisdom, through spirit totems, shrines, and other ways to manifest and connect with that energy. Some Pacific NW clan houses are entered through the mouth of Raven, as in their creation stories.*

Raven house
Gwayasdums, British Columbia

Pergola
Athens, Greece

Make place for community to grow. Community is born and its energy nurtured through many subtle things. A coffee shop or shady place to sit where news passes, friendships lubricate, and new things spark into being. The percentage of people on the street that we know and care about. Song. Hardship and joy shared. Passage of life together.

Tea shop, Kiyomizu-dera
Kyoto, Japan

Rialto Market
Venice, Italy

85

WHOLENESS

All parts of the cycles of life must be honored parts of our lives and surroundings if we are to know wholeness. Death, for example, is an essential and wonderful part of the cycles of life, and important to honor, not ignore, in our places. Out of death, the compost of one life, new life arises in ever greater richness. In celebrating the grief, and joy of death as well as life, a garden, a town - all things which we make - can add richness and meaning to our lives.

To spread the ashes of our loved ones and know that their material bodies will surround us still in the song of birds and the beauty of trees and flowers is a truly transformative experience. Our relationship with the places where we live and the nurture they can give us is deepened forever.

Death does not separate us from what is passed or is yet to come. Touch, honor, and listen to both, for they are part of what is now. Celebrate endings as well as beginnings in your life and work.

Resurrection Chapel
Turku, Finland

Crematory forest
Finland

Plains Indian burial scaffold

▲ *Simple shrouded burial in the ground, or burial scaffolds as used by Native Americans, allow our material bodies to become part of the rest of the living world, rather than to be kept isolated in hermetically sealed containers.*

◄ *A Finnish funeral chapel is similar to many churches, except that seating for the living is kept to one side of the church. The other is reserved for the dead, and for memorials to them. The side of the chapel behind the casket is a glass wall looking out into the forest. After a memorial service, the body or urn is carried out through a ceremonial portal into the forest for burial.*

Nurselog, Oregon

▲ *Once we honor death in our hearts, images of new life arising out of old suddenly become visible which can become part of our gardens as well as our natural surroundings.*

87

Entry
Neahkahnie, Oregon

▲ *Using natural materials rooted in the places where we build imparts a truth of meaning and connection to our places.*

TRUTH

We *can't* lie. All things touch. The connectedness that exists among all life on the energetic level means that we, and all else, are aware deep inside of the truth of everything we've ever been related to. There is reality to the Aboriginal saying, "We can't lie, because our minds are open and joined to each other."

Such connectedness and knowing of each other means we don't have to worry about our untruths returning to cripple us, cut us off from reality, and prevent us from acting truly and successfully. Connection means reality in the information we act on and the world we live into being. It means that we're not alone - that others can share what we feel, and witness our situation, and often even help us. Knowing each other more completely, we can more sensitively respond to each other's needs. It means deeper, richer, and more truthful relationships.

The freedom and beauty of the love that flows in such connection lets us experience true joy. It lets us know the plenitude of love we have to give in the rest of our lives. And acknowledging the truth of our inner voices reassures us of our own sanity in the craziness of the fantasy world we have built around us.

Surroundings which pretend to be what they aren't encompass us with untruthfulness - to the point we may have trouble remembering what truth is and what wisdom it communicates.

▶ *Letting the places we shape grow out of the truth of their situation rather than images of other times and places, they embrace us with a deep sense of rightness and beauty. Building down into the desert using the earth's own materials balances the hot days and cold nights, avoids strong winds, and bestows a sense of wisdom and rightness to our surroundings.*

Paolo Soleri's Cosanti Foundation
Tucson, Arizona

▶ *When we reconnect with the truth of the very diverse regions we live in, we celebrate that diversity with utterly unique and wonderful ways to build, live, and relate to and celebrate the specialness of each place.*

▶▶ *The support which a world without lies gives us brings an assurance, self-confidence, and rightness to our actions which echoes back onto us from the places we create.*

Door
Alquezar, Spain

Stairway
Neahkahnie, Oregon

89

BEING AT HOME

Quarry in winter
Fostoria, Ohio

W*e can sense the differentness of a culture based on understanding of our energetic nature and its relation to the sacred in the words of Malidoma Somé from THE HEALING WISDOM OF AFRICA:*

"Spirit and work are linked among indigenous people because human work is viewed as an intensification of the work that Spirit does in nature.....Individuals, as extensions of Spirit, come into the world with a purpose. At its core, the purpose of an individual is to bring beauty, harmony, and communion to Earth.

....Most work in the village is done collectively. The purpose is not so much the desire to get the job done but to raise enough energy for people to feel nourished by what they do. The nourishment does not come after the job, it comes before the job and during the job.....You are nourished first, and then the work flows out of your fullness.

As a result of our work practices, the indigenous notion of abundance is very different from that in the West. Villagers are interested not in accumulation but in a sense of fullness.....Abundance, in that sense of fullness, has a power that takes us away from worry."

Being "at home" is to know that fullness.

▼ *Entry requires a separate place to open into within a house, apart from all interior activities. It is an area inside that is still part of the public world, where we deal with strangers as well as family. Separation, not size, is important. A bookcase, portable screen, or even a curtain, can visually close off the entry from the rest of the interior.*

House entry
Neahkahnie, Oregon

WELCOME

Entries to places, particularly homes, hold an importance in the energy of place far beyond their actual size. Through them we can honor the ritual of arrivals and departures, in-between places and times, strangers and friends. They give place for memories, hopes, and dreams; tears, grief, passion, and fears - the true fires of life. They can show us how important it is to pay careful attention to each thing we do, and to learn to trust our tummies in the process. That is what tells us most directly whether we have comfort with a particular place. And that comfort is a measure of how deeply we are in harmony with our world.

Bed and Breakfast
Manzanita, Oregon

▶ *Small, visually insignificant things can be very important to our comfort. The location of a doorbell may confuse the boundaries between public and private areas. A gate in the fence here originally led up to a door in the glassed-in porch - obviously used as part of the house. Do we go on in and ring the doorbell at the original front door? Or will the owner open the door and say, "What are you doing in my house?" Here, relocation of the gate and entry walk directs people to the door being used for entry.*

Entries can also be a place of *giving* - offering shade, coolness and water in the heat; warmth and shelter in the cold. They can be a place of giving to the street....of beauty, of caring, of connection and conversation; of guardians and a watchful eye; of mingling the emotions and energies of family and community. They can be places of *honoring* - honoring visitors and guests, honoring the neighborhood, nature, the materials whose lives were given up in the making of the place.

Entries are settings for important occurrences in our lives. Passionate goodnights after a date, farewells, waiting for family or friends to return, setting off to school or work, return to comfort and rest at the end of a day. They define sacred space. They become containers for ritual energy, adding power to those rituals. Most of these things require *at least* an eddy out of the way of traffic in and out of an entry door. Some require much more.

▶ *Shelter, warmth, food, and companionship regardless of the worst of weather. The wood is dry, the larder full - a haven in any storm. True welcome!*

Porch and entry
Neahkahnie, Oregon

93

Building blocks
Neahkhanie, Oregon

▲ *Television dominates the energetics of our homes, and weakens our self-esteem. As we replace it with more participatory activities, we dramatically enhance the energetics of home. Homes should nurture our growth.*

INSIDE HOMES

Homes are very personal places. Our individual living patterns, cultural traditions, and comfort levels vary immensely. The energetics of personal space are dominated by our hearts and minds. Glare, noise, smells affect us differently. What represents comfort, security, and pleasure to each of us is vastly different, and it is those personal perceptions that need satisfaction. Listening to our tummies as to what feels good or bad to us is vital.

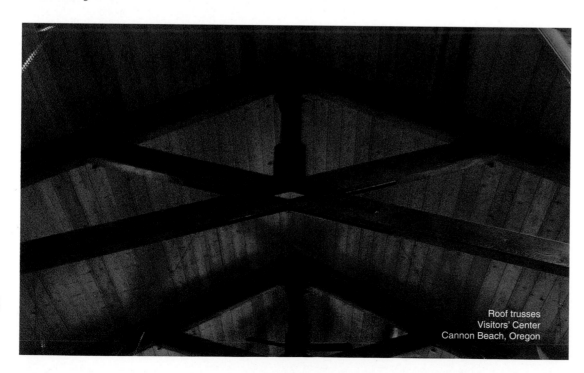

Roof trusses
Visitors' Center
Cannon Beach, Oregon

◀ *Our sense of the adequacy of our shelter affects our comfort. Fears of the roof blowing off in a storm silently saps our energy. Worry about a sagging floor or beam, or a leaking roof diffuses our attention. Assurance that our home will meet our needs of shelter gives peace of mind and creates a true sanctuary.*

Dining room
Minneapolis, Minnesota

Bedroom window seat
Neahkahnie, Oregon

▲ *Many homes are overwhelmed by our belongings. Clearing out old "stuff" and dealing with clutter is like weeding a garden. It opens space and light for new things to grow in our lives and for us to focus on what is truly important. Things which needlessly divert our attention keep us from our true goals. Arranging space use so we aren't unexpectedly intruded upon releases our subconscious to concentrate fully on other things.*

◄ *Doors and windows are "in-between spaces". Enlarging that edge into a realm of its own, with porches, verandahs, window seats, and entries, can create comfort in our complex world. Steps can give a place to sit when unsure whether we want to be out or in, letting us be part of both. A window seat can allow us to linger securely inside our home, yet able to call out to a neighbor or friend or just enjoy the passing world.*

95

Bed alcove
Neahkahnie, Oregon

EVERYDAY SACRED

Every part of the daily patterns in our homes contains opportunity for embodying the sacred in our lives, for honoring others, finding meaning in our lives, and for deepening our rootedness with the rest of our cosmos. The patterns we choose strongly affect the nature of our energy and health and that with which our surroundings enfold us.

A good servant is invisible - a presence known only through the smooth and faultless orchestration of energy, communication, and flow of experience.

▲ *Where and how we sleep is personal and ever-changing. What is more important is what we wake to and say goodnight to, where and how we dream, and whose hands we put ourselves into when we sleep. The place between asleep and awake is a place where the veils to the spirit world are thin and where our dreams can be brought to life.*

96

Garden and pool
Rose Valley, Pennsylvania

◄ *"Living-room" is seed of family and community. It is catalyst for enabling and evoking our relationships, honoring others, those relationships, and ourselves. It is a place of opportunity to care, to give gifts of spirit, hope, love, and support. It may be indoors or out, a kitchen, a bed, a garden, or even a doorstep.*

When our places act as good servants, they keep our focus on people, community, other life, and interaction - not on themselves. They place but small demands on us for attention, operation and maintenance. They evoke deep and moving experiences. They become known only slowly.....revealing quiet surprises to us from time to time. They surround us only with meaningful things, and convey love and clarity of intention. They make us subtly aware of important things in life, so we can come to feel at home everywhere.

Bathroom
Manzanita, Oregon

Kitchen
Neahkahnie, Oregon

▲ *A bath can be the heart of a home - a place to honor and restore our bodies and our spirits, to wash off the fatigue and tensions of the day, and find wholeness out of its experiences. Our bodies, too, are sacred and wonderful. Even our wastes are food for other life, and nutrients that need to return to the fields.*

▲ *A good kitchen does not need fancy appliances, or cabinets filled with equipment and packaged foods. It needs to be a place capable of honoring and enabling those who feed and care for others. It needs to cradle the social rituals of making meals. It needs to honor the foods, allow them to embody the energy given through them by the cook, and enhance their ability to nurture our energy as well as our bodies.*

MIRRORS

Mirrors distort. Every morning they reinforce a vision of ourselves at our bleary-eyed, rumpled worst. They destroy self-esteem or base it on cosmetic appearances. They focus our attention on outer appearances rather than inner realities - in both ourselves and others. Without mirrors nudging our consciousness of externals, we think less about ourselves, stop being so concerned with the outside packaging of people and things, and become more attuned and responsive to important qualities within.

Mirrors are a minor part of our homes. Yet getting rid of mirrors can do wonders for our spirits and the spirit of our buildings.

▼ *Mirrors in unexpected places (here under the floor of a play structure) can tweak our hearts and minds by reflecting different juxtapositions and contexts.*

▼ *Mirrors cause us to forget that all things reflect the values, dreams, and fears of their makers. Our places reflect only what we are. They cannot touch the earth until we do.*

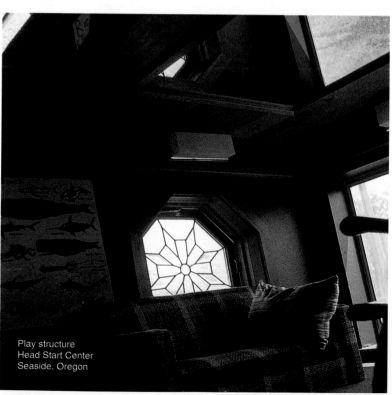

Play structure
Head Start Center
Seaside, Oregon

Cliff Palace Village
Mesa Verde, Colorado

▶ *A window instead of a mirror over a bathroom sink can connect us to a garden instead of reminding us of a hangover. Mirrors can be put inside a closet or medicine cabinet door, or on the back of a bathroom door until needed.*

Bathroom
Neahkahnie, Oregon

99

Guest loft under tree
Neahkahnie, Oregon

100

THE
COMMUNITY
OF LIFE

A building is enriched and given meaning when it brings us into closer touch with each other, the rest of the world, and the rhythms of nature. By opening our places to sunrise, moonset, and the stars; to the daily and seasonal cycles of life; to the beauty of rain, fog and snow; to spiders and butterflies, we deepen our connection to the rest of our visible and invisible universe.

Our homes can help us keep our hearts open. They can embody and surround us with love and community, and maintain our connection with the rest of life. They need to be an emotionally safe place where we can open ourselves to the energy from the rest of Creation that nurtures our lives.

◀ *A place open to the sky can connect us to the cycles of the sun, moon, stars, and rain.*

Tatsumura Silk Mansion
Kyoto, Japan

▲
▼ *The places we live in can shelter us from difficult conditions, when needed, without separating us from the rest of the world of which we are part.*

▼ *To be at home in a place, we need to nestle in and become part of the unique community of life that has evolved in it. This wildflower meadow emerged and nestled in around the home on its own merely from an indecision of whether to plant a lawn.*

Living room
Neahkahnie, Oregon

Wildflower meadow
Neahkahnie, Oregon

101

8

THE PLACE OF SPIRIT

Pollen on water
Smith Rocks SP, Oregon

Our own culture's separation from operating in the realms of chi and the sacred is fairly recent, and the membrane which separates us from that world is paper-thin and easy to penetrate. Attending services in a Christian church, we can see everywhere practices that were originally based in working with chi. In baptism ceremonies there are often ritual actions of touching the crown of the head (crown chakra) and the middle of the forehead (third eye chakra) with Holy Water, and an "opening of the eyes". The hand positions in blessings by a minister or priest echo those used for millennia in radiating healing or nurturing chi from the palms. Rituals of consecration of a new church mirror almost word for word those used in moving chi energy in place in dozens of cultures. Faith-healing in Pentecostal Churches is based on chi energy.

Because we've believed that chi doesn't exist, these actions have lacked both strength of belief and use of the simple techniques needed to actually tap into and activate chi. The result is something like a child "talking" on a phone but not knowing they need to plug in or dial up.

"Plugging-in" to chi is easy. It requires centering, grounding, opening the chakras and "dialing-up" a long-distance connection to whatever we are seeking. Then real conversations and true energy can flow between us, others, and the web of life that surrounds us.

SACREDNESS

Places, as well as people, draw sustenance from how they are held in our hearts. We need to hold places sacred, because we need to hold ourselves and all else sacred in order to be whole. We need *special* sacred places because we need to be able to touch the immensity of power in nature, and the energetic roots of events and beliefs which we value.

Sacred places forge and strengthen bonds between us and the universe in which we believe. They empower us by affirming the wholeness of the universe we see revealed about us, and by reflecting our chosen place and role in that universe. If our surroundings show only the scars and ravages of greed, that will become the heart of our community. If we ensure that our surroundings show reverence for all Creation, our communities can see alternatives upon which to chart their futures.

The role of focal places, such as shrines, is important to the function that *chi* plays in generating and sustaining the power of people and places. They converge and concentrate that energy and increase our ability to connect with it.

It is *our* act of frankly affirming and acknowledging sacredness, and opening ourselves to the connectedness which it engenders, which becomes enshrined in a sacred place. Our *act* of holding sacred is root, not where or how we choose to carry out that act. It is *that* which empowers and transforms us, the shrines and sacred places, and our communities.

Everglades National Park, Florida

◀ Until we visit a national wildlife preserve, we might think our society doesn't create shrines. The sound and beauty of the teeming life there can be incredibly joyful. But beneath that sound, and even more wonderful, is the fact that we have held other life sacred and inviolate. We have created a sacred place.....as far as the eye can see.

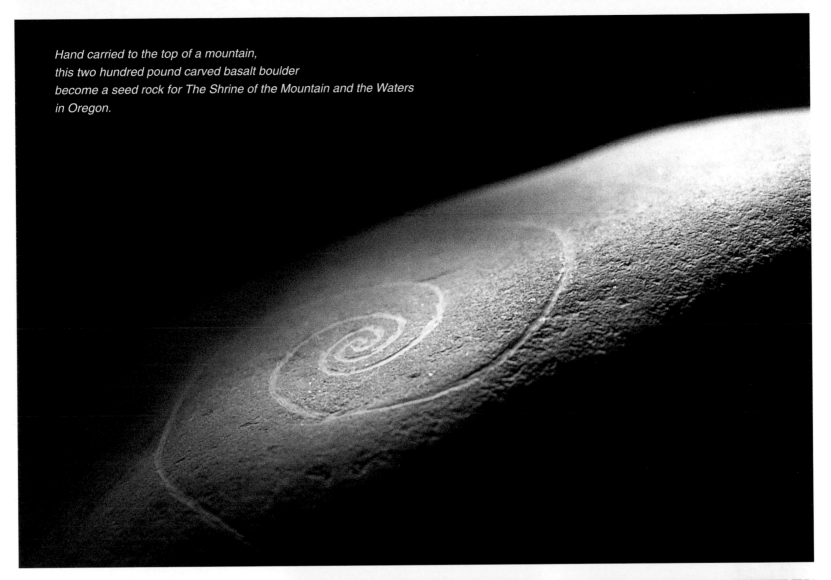

*Hand carried to the top of a mountain,
this two hundred pound carved basalt boulder
become a seed rock for The Shrine of the Mountain and the Waters
in Oregon.*

▶ *A sacred place in our homes honors our beliefs
and triggers the grounding and nurturing of our own
energy. A small corner in our homes filled with clear
intention can affirm and anchor the sacred in our
lives.*

▶ ▶ *Our neighborhoods need places of silence - to
meditate, to find a moment of peace, or to restore
our energy in deeper and more powerful ways.
Special, powerful, sacred places can serve our
entire communities.*

Bedroom shrine
Neahkahnie, Oregon

Kami shrine
Muroji Shrine, Japan

105

Masks in ritual and ceremony separate us from our conventional world and help us open to the spirit of the lifeform we assume. That new awareness carries on into our subsequent actions.

Carnival mask
Venice, Italy

SPIRIT TOTEMS

Every form of life is a different facet of the jewel of Creation and has particular characteristics which distinguish it. Those attributes give it unique perceptions, powers, and relationships with the rest of existence.

Through trance, mimicry, and opening psychically to these different lives, we can enter within and experience their unique nexus of the universe and even assume some of their powers. This ability to connect with all Creation on

Temple guardian
Horyuji Temple, Japan

◀ *The fierce figures located in the gateways to Japanese temples embody shielding protection of those within connecting with the spirit world.*

▶ *Native Americans in the Pacific Northwest work and live closely with spirit totems in all of their art, aspecting their nature with compelling masks and dance, and imbuing their dwellings with the embodied power and imagery of the family totems.*

106

Haida "Bear Mother" housepost
British Columbia

the energetic level and in the spirit world deepens our resonance and harmony with the song of life, and enriches the wisdom with which we move through life.

Other cultures live intimately with and commune continually with this world and these powers. This depth of experience and relationship with other life transforms our existence, giving immense richness of meaning and knowing to our actions and a community of support for all.

The carved eagle on the ridge beam of this living room combine with the materials of the ceiling to give a forceful sense of being protectively sheltered under the wings of a bird.

Eagle-sheltered roof
Portland, Oregon

Aiyedakun Yoruba Shrine
Ontoto, Nigeria

◀ *Susanne Wenger's expressive Yoruba shrines give potent imagery to the spirits connected with them. The mouth, trunk, and ears of an elephant, transformed by the passion of the orisha, are visible under the roof.*

▶ *A place of sanctuary and shelter is promised by the sculpted images greeting us at the gateway.*

Entry portal sculpture
Notre Dame Cathedral
Paris, France

107

Palm frond wedding decorations
Borobudur Village, Java

LIVING ART

All things and places we create are *living*, and require nurture. They live not alone but in community, and flows of energy between us and them give to both. All things live through the reverence with which we hold them. A cathedral is sustained by the living faith of its community. Without that faith, it crumbles to pieces - unloved, unmaintained, abandoned and destroyed. Without being nurtured itself, a place has nothing to give to those whose lives it must support, and we fall in turn into the same dereliction.

Places retain the reverberations of events long past that have occurred in them. The cumulative patina from those events adds to the power of a place to affect our lives.

▲ *In ceremonial art, we acknowledge the primacy of the energetic, creative, inner product of the work. But the same importance lies in that aspect of our making, using, and maintaining of enduring places. Without that ongoing nurture, our places become only dusty, inert and ignored relics of the past. Like plastic flowers on a grave, it can be as wrong to make things permanent whose role is a token of giving, remembrance, or celebration. Part of the vital act of ritual is ceremonial involvement in the making of impermanent material trappings.*

Gardening has always been a living art. Plants grow, and die, and over years and centuries a garden's composition changes, even when seeking to retain the same spirit. But gardening without sacredness lets wither the energetic level of existence sustained through loving care. Lacking that, many of the deeply moving Zen gardens in Japan have died in the last thirty years.

This one still has living energy, sustained through the ongoing creative work of its caregivers.

Ryogen-in
Kyoto, Japan

▶ The energetic life of a place must be sustained as attentively as its physical existence. Installation of loudspeakers for tour guides can destroy the serenity of a garden, block its ability to touch our hearts, and leave it a mere backdrop for tourist photographs.

Ryoanji Zen Garden
Kyoto, Japan

109

SACRED WORK

There are inner as well as outer products to all the work we do. The inner joy of discovering or perfecting skills, or of creating something of beauty can be more important than the outer results we expect.

The goal of singing a song is not to reach the end as quickly as possible. It is a state of creating harmony, beauty, growth, and understanding. The goal of work, as a sacred act, is to use the need for a product or service to develop the greatest possible power in the object, the makers, and the users.

Sacred work recognizes and demonstrates a threefold nature of creating - the application and enhancement of our skills and understanding, overcoming of self-centeredness through the coming together in common tasks, and the creation of things necessary for a becoming existence. It is a means of restoring wholeness to our lives and our minds. Work gives purchase to our dreams and disciplines our minds to purpose, value and meaning. Physical work puts the mind in service to the reality of the physical world. Sacred work puts the mind in service to the heart as well.   Sacred work acts upon, enhances, and enriches the wholeness of the web of life within which each thing is embedded, without rending the fabric of its wholeness.

Naiku Shrine
Ise, Japan

◄ Over 1400 years of sacred work at Ise Shrine has imbued every stone of it with such purity and mindfulness of action and understanding of worker, tool, material and purpose that it draws the breath away in awe. It is a process that provides ongoing sustenance for the spiritual power of the builders as well as the building.

Entry gate
Neahkahnie, Oregon

Notre Dame Cathedral
Paris, France

▲ The perfection of work in the hidden parts of the
Gothic cathedrals, "known only by its maker and
God", was the result of work considered both as an
offering and as a path to inner growth

◄ It does not take the
skill of a Zen master or
the budget of an
Emperor to create
magic. Any of the
tasks we each have
before us offer
opportunity for sacred
work and its product.

*Deep skill remains almost invisible
until we grasp the profundity
of the task attempted.*

Stairs
Eikando Temple
Kyoto, Japan

111

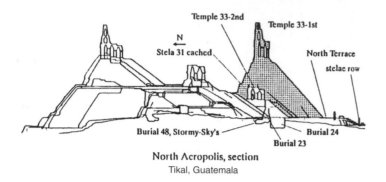

Temple 33-2nd   Temple 33-1st

N

Stela 31 cached   North Terrace
                    stelae row

Burial 48, Stormy-Sky's   Burial 24
          Burial 23

North Acropolis, section
Tikal, Guatemala

◀ *The great Mayan centers in Mesoamerica created ways for shared experience of the energy of the spirit world through public ritual, trance, dance, and aspecting of ancestors and gods. Their layered construction reflects sequences of reaffirmation and adjustment of their design as portals to the spirit world that have occurred over time. The cumulative energy of that intention has given such places great power.*

Naga railing
Angkor Wat, Cambodia

PORTALS TO THE SPIRIT WORLD

Past and future, ancestors and descendants, what preceded and what evolves from our lives coexist and are accessible through the energetics of place.

Through ritual or design, places come to act as a nexus or portal between the everyday world and the realms of energy and spirit. Such places assist intuitive communicative abilities, provide safe and supportive environments for accessing those worlds, hold the energy of linkage between realms, and give form to those domains in our material world. Acknowledging chi is bringing a whole new understanding of the function of temples, shrines, and other facilities of different cultures.

◀ *Funerary temples such as Angkor Wat in Cambodia were energetically designed to act as places of access to deceased leaders still existing in their energetic bodies, assisting the ability of their descendants and their subjects to continue to access their wisdom and aid. Energized sculpture of nagas represent the seven chakras of our bodies' chi network.*

Face towers, Bayon
Angkor Thom, Cambodia

◀ *The sculpted heads of the central Bayon temple, the city gates, and other shrines in Angkor, with their eyes half-closed in meditation, were part of an immense symbolic and energetic system of manifesting and distributing chi energy throughout the kingdom. This chi was channeled from the energy dimensions of existence to the material one through the king, in trance, in his sacred role.*

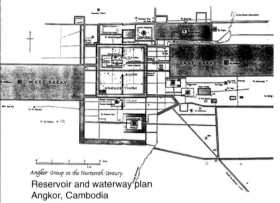

Angkor Group in the Fourteenth Century
Reservoir and waterway plan
Angkor, Cambodia

▲ *The Khmers created a framework encompassing, enfolding, and transforming the entire material world of the kingdom. Every part of a Khmer's surroundings functioned to connect and empower them through their spiritual/governmental system. Wherever one was - on roadways, canals, levees, in fields, towns, between temples and reservoirs - one was surrounded by and within that framework. That framework or connection system manifested the spiritual world within the material one and brought the material one into full congruence with the energetic/spiritual one.*

113

There are songs in stone as well as in sound, which overflow with rejoicing at the bountiful richness of Creation

AT HOME WITH THE SACRED

For us to be truly at home in a place, it must contain silence, song, and shadows. We need silence to hear the wordless voices that speak to us directly from all life. We need silence to be free from the words that come between us and reality. We need silence to still our chattering minds and focus on the new creation to which we are constantly giving birth. There is a music to silence and a dance within stillness which is lacking in our lives and communities.

We need song - to reflect and catalyze our resonance with the other voices of life, and to give voice and wings to joy, grief, ecstasy and sorrow. We need song to give our thanks for the wondrous Creation of which we are part.

And we need shadows, for they harbor the unknown and the unknowable. We need shadows to see inward rather than to look only outward. We need shadows for room to breathe and space to wonder. Without darkness, there is no light, and we would not know stars.

▼ *Elimination of the noise of refrigerators, furnaces, TVs, and the other machinery common to our homes allows a wonderful silence to emerge and be filled with the sound of birds, wind in the trees, and rain on the roof.*

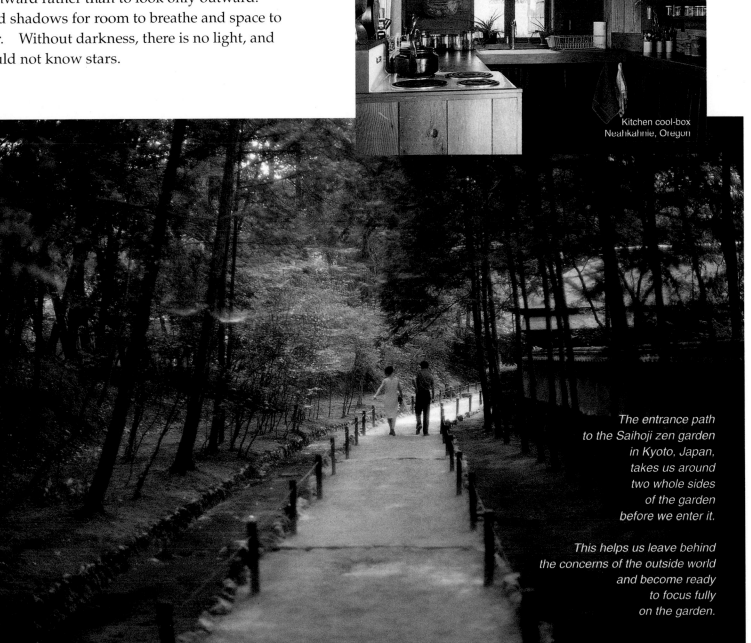

Kitchen cool-box
Neahkahnie, Oregon

The entrance path to the Saihoji zen garden in Kyoto, Japan, takes us around two whole sides of the garden before we enter it.

This helps us leave behind the concerns of the outside world and become ready to focus fully on the garden.

Dilwara Temple
Mt. Abu, India

PUTTING LOVE
INTO A
PLACE

Garden
Tatsamura Silk Mansion
Kyoto, Japan

Entry door, Timberline Lodge
Mt. Hood, Oregon

Carved roof beams
Portland, Oregon

At root, what really matters
concerning the spirit of place
and the place of spirit
is that we act from love
in all we do.

All else comes forth from that.

Window seat
Turku Castle
Turku, Finland

117

9

ALL THINGS IN TURN

Morning fog
Shrine of the Mountain and the Waters
Neahkahnie Mt., Oregon.

A garden of breezes.

Prayer flags
Neahkahnie, Oregon.

We can begin to see now how a chi-centered world changes every facet of our surroundings and our lives. Those changes run deep inside us and our world, causing our communities to become very different places to live.

While some transformations are dramatic, others occur quietly, like the succession from an alder to a coniferous forest. One day we see only the fast-growth alder colonizers. Then slowly the conifers grow up, inch by inch, between the alders. As the alders rot and die out, one day we find we are in the midst of a mature coniferous forest. Like such a forest, we have today two cultures occupying the same place - a new and enduring one coming into maturity, the other reaching its end. A change from focusing on the unraveling of the old to bringing forth and seeing the wonders emerging with the new can fill our lives with new purpose and joy.

The transformation to sustainability required of us in the coming decades will bring major changes. Part of these changes involve the design principles of energetics of place. It is up to us to integrate them as a touchstone and core to our design arts to give them the wholeness and depth needed to express and manifest these new visions and values.

What we are likely to see in the next decades depends in part on what we can "see" within what surrounds us today. Many things will be as striking in their absence as in their presence.

Instead of being segregated as today, an intimate interweaving of work place, living place, leisure and learning will be more common - eliminating much of today's demand for daily mobility. Restoration of the beauty and power of communities and natural places will be actively sought, as people work to "make where they *are* paradise" rather than needing to escape to "recreate" in better places.

Being hypnotized by mobility and its attendant freeways, ubiquitous automobiles, and ceaseless aircraft takeoffs and landings will be a thing of the past. This is in part because of the depletion of cheap fossil fuels which underlie current mobility. But more importantly, it will be a response to a realization that mobility makes all places alike, destroying its own value. We will findgreatly expanded, comfortable, and convenient transit, high-speed trains, and neighborhood-based rental vehicles. People will still be moving, living, and traveling around the world. But they are likely to be on slower *pilgrimages* more deeply involved in learning from and sharing with others instead of short and frequent trips.

Urban skylines of towering office buildings will similarly become less common as sedentary and unrewarding office work is replaced by more active involvement with local production of needed goods and services. Billboards and advertising will virtually vanish as we come to see them as an expensive and wasteful goads to excessive consumption. We will experience an interest in quality and meaning, instead of quantity and "appearances".

Gardening and learning
Rose Valley, Pennsylvania

The twenty-first century community will likely be smaller, with longtime residents, as the importance of intimacy in interaction with people and place becomes felt and as the higher effectiveness of local production for local needs becomes vital. There will be a quiet, unhurried air to the patterns of life, as the walls between work and leisure are removed and the immense costs in time and production needed for today's growth are eliminated. We will find people on the street connecting with us, interested in us, and interesting *to* us in turn. We may find only remnants of the large-scale institutions such as the prisons, schools, hospitals, shopping centers, power stations, and airports that have today replaced direct dealing with our needs.

Radio, TV, sports, music, and other cultural media will be transformed, as we rediscover that *doing* is far more rewarding than passively watching others perform. Paradoxically, the interest in and attention to professional performances will be more intense and involved as more people are observing out of their own competence rather than as just couch potatoes.

What we may most surprisingly find, is that these apparently isolated communities are even more deeply and intensively interconnected in global and interest communities as well. We will be pleased to find that the level of well-being, satisfaction, security, as well as our physical, spiritual and emotional health, far exceed those of today.

These profound changes in the *what, where,* and *how* of our activities will likely be equaled by the changes in architecture, landscape, interior, and urban design. While new building activity will dramatically lessen as our population stabilizes, the modification, replacement, and upgrading of existing facilities will result in an architecture and communities with distinctive regional character, which are able to touch our hearts. Local materials, local climate responses, daylighting, solar heating, night cooling, and native landscaping will produce remarkable character changes from one region to another.

The reworking of our existing urban fabric from a new value base will transform our communities, and imbue them with positive characteristics virtually absent in today's cities. One focus will be on improving the "chi" already existing in natural and built places and creating places with healthy "chi" for all people and all life. There will be more places that evoke community intimacy. We wil have places filled with the powerful in-breath of silence. Our communities will have places to nurture the soul as well as shelter the body.

They will also both accommodate and represent healthful and nurturing work that enhances our skills and produces the goods and services needed for a healthy existence. They will reflect the values of giving, caring, equity, durability, and respect for all creation, and will hold all of that creation sacred. They will create space so the spirits of our air, land, and waters may flow free again. And most of all they will express the gift of love going into the making of places, and the passion of that uninhibited giving of love.

We have discovered already that this new operative vision *does* produce a new architecture, a new landscape, and new communities. It *does* produce places with souls, ones that can move our hearts, and ones that honor and accommodate all of Creation. And it does this while enriching rather than destroying our planet and our souls in the process. With that in our hearts, a wonderful healing and a new era of our world can begin.

Entry garden
Neahkahnie, Oregon

Our spirits don't require roofs for shelter and walls for protection. They do require honoring, sanctuary, and nurture. Gardens for our spirits can provide us with needed revitalization and growth between bouts of dealing with the world.

121

SOURCES AND RESOURCES

ILLUSTRATIONS:

Photographs, other than noted below, are by the author.
Projects shown from Oregon represent the author's work integrating energetics of place into contemporary architectural practice.

Principal sources for other images, drawings and text, or accessible information on the material presented are:

p 16 - *I-Ching*, Richard Wilhelm translation, Princeton Univ. Press, 1950; p18 - *The Imperial Travelling Palace at the Hoo-kew-shan*, CHINA, Vol 1, Thomas Allom; p20 - *reconstruction of Puabi's Headdress*, Sumeria, courtesy of University of Pennsylvania Museum; p21 - *Earth's Magnetosphere* - courtesy of The National Geographical Society; p26 - *Grave, Fuchou, Fukien Province, China*, BAUKUNST UND LANDSCHAFT IN CHINA, Ernst Boerschmann; p31 - *Maya vision serpent*, A FOREST OF KINGS, Linda Schele and David Freidel, courtesy of the author; p32 - *Acupuncture meridians*, see ACUPUNCTURE, Felix Mann, 1978; p33 - *Chakras*, see YOGA: THE METHOD OF REINTEGRATON, Alain Danielou, 1949; p34 - *Space and Time Geometries*, PRINCIPLES OF COMPOSITION IN HINDU SCULPTURE, Alice Boner; p36 - *Hawaiian birth stones* - photo by Kathleen Bender; *Temple Mandala* - based upon Archeological Survey of India drawings, see LIVING ARCHITECTURE - INDIAN, Andreas Volwahsen; p37 - *Diorite statue of Pharaoh Chephren*, Cairo Museum;

p41 - *Dowsing EEGs* - Dowser's Brainwave Research Project, Ed Stillman and Dr. Matthew J. Kelly, courtesy of The American Society of Dowsers, PO Box 24, Danville VT, 05828; p43 - *Crow on Pine*, Niten, see THE ART AND ARCHITECTURE OF JAPAN, Paine & Sopher; p54 - *3600 ft. long megalithic beam bridge in Fukien Prov., China, 1053 A.D.*, HISTOIRE DES ARTS ANCIENS DE LA CHINE, Vol. 4, Osvald Siren or SCIENCE AND CIVILIZATION IN CHINA, Vol. 4, Joseph Needham; p55 - *Loess road, China*, see Boerschmann; p60 - *Chess Pavilion, Huashan*, see LIVING ARCHITECTURE - CHINESE, Michele Pirazzoli-T'Serstevens, courtesy of Camera Press; *Energetic surveys of Dendera and Chartres*, POINTS OF COSMIC ENERGY, Blanche Merz; p62 - *Construction of 7 circuit labyrinth*, LABYRINTHS, Sig Lonegren; *Borobudur model*, see TEMPLES OF SOUTHEAST ASIA, *Louis-Frederic, 1965; Chartres labyrinth* - See Merz or Lonegren; p70 - *Taos Pueblo*, photo by Kathleen Bender;

p71 - *Isfahan plan*, see PERSIAN GARDENS AND GARDEN PAVILIONS, Donald Wilber; *Chang'an plan*, see Pirazzoli-T'Serstevens; p75 - *Barn raising*, photo by Liz Beckman; p77 - *Hasht Behesht*, Pascal Coste, see Wilber; p78 - *Adalej well section*, Archeological Survey of India, via FORMAL STRUCTURE IN INDIAN ARCHITECTURE exhibition, Klaus Herdeg; p84 - *Raven house, Gwayasdums Kwakiutl village*, courtesy Royal British Columbia Museum, and p87 - *Plains Indian burial scaffold*, O.S. Goff, see NATIVE AMERICAN ARCHITECTURE, Peter Nabokov & Robert Easton; p91 - *THE HEALING WISDOM OF AFRICA, Malidoma Somé*; p96 - *Garden*, photo by Lane deMoll; p106 -*Venice mask* - photo by Skye Bender-deMoll; p106 *Haida house post*, see Nabokov & Easton; p107 - *Aiyedakun, Yoruba shrine by Suzanne Wenger*, see RETURN OF THE GODS, Ulli Beier; p112 - *Section, north acropolis at Tikal*, see Schele & Freidel, courtesy of the author; p113 - *Plan, Angkor, Cambodia*, after Viktor Golobew, see ANGKOR, Bernard Grosslier; p120 - *Gardening*, photo by Lane deMoll.

FURTHER READING ON ENERGETICS OF PLACE:

INTRODUCTION TO FENG-SHUI
Stephan D.R. Feuchtwang - AN ANTHROPOLOGICAL ANALYSIS OF CHINESE GEOMANCY, Vithagna, 1974.
  Still one of the few resources to cover the breadth of feng shui traditions.
Lam Kam Chuen - FENG SHUI HANDBOOK, Henry Holt, 1996.
  A good general introduction to traditional feng-shui practices.
Gill Hale - THE FENG SHUI GARDEN, Story Books, 1998.
  A good introduction to a feng-shui approach to gardening.

RECONCEPTUALIZING A WORLD OF ENERGETICS
Machaelle Small Wright - CO-CREATIVE SCIENCE, Perelandra, 1997.
  Theory of direct, active, and personal partnership between us and nature for working together to successfully address problems. 800-960-8806
Machaelle Small Wright - PERELANDRA GARDEN WORKBOOK, 2nd Ed., Perelandra, 1993. Communication, working with, co-creative processes, energetic dimensions of gardens and life. (See also Workbook II)
Barbara Hand Clow - THE PLEIADIAN AGENDA, Bear & Co., 1995
  Pretty weird, I would have said a year ago. Maybe now, maybe not. Good for loosening our sense of the possible.

THE ENERGETICS OF COMMUNITY
Starhawk - THE FIFTH SACRED THING, Bantam, 1993.
  A beautiful image of the world we may be converging onto, and the power of the spirit in it.
Malidoma Somé - THE HEALING WISDOM OF AFRICA, Tarcher/Putnam, 1998. Ritual, work, healing, and community in a spirit-centered culture.
Malidoma Somé OF WATER AND THE SPIRIT, Tarcher/Putnam, 1994.
  Powerful autobiography - life in contemporary African tribal culture - spirit world, community energy.
David Freidel, Linda Schele, and Joy Parker - MAYA COSMOS: Three Thousand Years on the Shaman's Path, Wm. Morrow & Co., 1993. The role of shamanism in the Maya culture.
Blanche Merz POINTS OF COSMIC ENERGY, C.W. Daniel. 1987.
  Dowsing research into energetics of sacred sites of various cultures.
Robert Lawlor VOICES OF THE FIRST DAY: Awakening in the Aboriginal Dreamtime, Inner Traditions International, 1991.
  As the title says.

WORKING WITH AND USING ENERGY
Joey Korn - DOWSING: A PATH TO ENLIGHTENMENT, 1997.
  Moving and changing energy in our surroundings. 706-733-0204
Barbara Brennan, HANDS OF LIGHT, Bantam Books, 1987. Outstanding introduction to chi energy in the body.
Donna Eden, ENERGY MEDICINE, Tarcher/Putnam, 1998.
  Energy testing, and the systems of energy in our bodies.
Carolyn Myss, ANATOMY OF THE SPIRIT, Harmony Books, 1996. The sacred, bodily energetics, and our health.
Denise Linn - SACRED SPACE, Ballantine Books, 1995. Clearing and enhancing the energy of your home.
Machaelle Small Wright - PERELANDRA GARDEN WORKBOOK II, Perelandra, 1990. Energy processes for co-creation with nature intelligences, co-existence with microbes, insects, and other forms of life. (See also Workbook I)
Jacques Lusseyran - AND THERE WAS LIGHT, Parabola, 1987.
  A blind French freedom fighter in WWII, and learnng to see with inner light.

FIRE RIVER PRESS
Quick Order Form

Telephone Inquiries: (503) 368-6294
Email Inquiries: fireriverpress@nehalemtel.net
Postal Orders: *FIRE RIVER PRESS*, PO Box 397, Manzanita OR 97130
Please send payment with orders.

PLEASE SEND THE FOLLOWING BOOKS:

_____

_____

_____

SHIPPING: US – $4 FOR THE FIRST BOOK, $2 FOR EACH ADDITIONAL BOOK.
INTERNATIONAL – $9 FOR FIRST BOOK, $5 FOR EACH ADDITIONAL BOOK. (ESTIMATE)

NAME: _____

ADDRESS: _____

CITY: _____ STATE: _____ ZIP: _____ COUNTRY: _____

TELEPHONE: _____ E-MAIL ADDRESS: _____

FIRE RIVER PRESS
Quick Order Form

Telephone Inquiries: (503) 368-6294
Email Inquiries: fireriverpress@nehalemtel.net
Postal Orders: *FIRE RIVER PRESS*, PO Box 397, Manzanita OR 97130
Please send payment with orders.

PLEASE SEND THE FOLLOWING BOOKS:

_____

_____

_____

SHIPPING: US – $4 FOR THE FIRST BOOK, $2 FOR EACH ADDITIONAL BOOK.
INTERNATIONAL – $9 FOR FIRST BOOK, $5 FOR EACH ADDITIONAL BOOK. (ESTIMATE)

NAME: _____

ADDRESS: _____

CITY: _____ STATE: _____ ZIP: _____ COUNTRY: _____

TELEPHONE: _____ E-MAIL ADDRESS: _____